Emerging Trends in Real Estate®

2015

Contents

Editorial Leadership Team

Emerging Trends Chairs
Mitchell M. Roschelle, PwC
Kathleen B. Carey, Urban Land Institute

Authors
Hugh F. Kelly
Andrew Warren, PwC

Principal Researchers and Advisers
Stephen Blank, Urban Land Institute
Anita Kramer, Urban Land Institute

Senior Advisers
Christopher J. Potter, PwC, Canada
Miriam Gurza, PwC, Canada
Susan M. Smith, PwC

ULI Editorial and Production Staff
James A. Mulligan, Senior Editor
David James Rose, Managing Editor/Manuscript Editor
Betsy VanBuskirk, Creative Director
Anne Morgan, Cover Design
Deanna Pineda, Muse Advertising Design, Designer
Craig Chapman, Senior Director of Publishing Operations
Xiaoning Mao, Project Intern

Emerging Trends in Real Estate® is a trademark of PwC and is registered in the United States and other countries. All rights reserved.

PwC firms help organizations and individuals create the value they're looking for. We're a network of firms in 158 countries with close to 169,000 people who are committed to delivering quality in assurance, tax, and advisory services. Tell us what matters to you and find out more by visiting us at www.pwc.com.

Learn more about PwC by following us online: @PwC_LLP, YouTube, LinkedIn, Facebook, and Google+.

Recommended bibliographic listing:

PwC and the Urban Land Institute: *Emerging Trends in Real Estate®* *2015*. Washington, D.C.: PwC and the Urban Land Institute, 2014.

ISBN: 978-0-87420-355-7

PwC Advisers and Contributing Researchers

Adam Boutros*	Jay Weinberg
Adam S. Feuerstein	Jeff Kiley
Adriane Bookwalter	Jeffrey Nasser
Aki Dellaportas	Jerry Kavanagh*
Allen Baker*	Jill Lising
Allen Topaloglu*	Jim D'Amore
Alysha Brady	John Amman
Amanda Gruskos	Jorja Mathers
Amy E. Olson	Judy Leung*
Amy Perron*	Julia Powell
Andrew Alperstein	Ken Griffin
Andrew Popert*	Kent Goetjen
Andrew Stansfield	Kevin King*
Andrew Warren	Kevin Nishioka
Brad Wood	Kourosh HoorAzar
Brett Matzek	Kristen Anderson
Bud Thomas	Kristen Conner
Carlo Bruno	Laura Daniels*
Chris Dietrick	Lori-Ann Beausoleil*
Chris Mill	Louis DeFalco
Chris Vangou*	Matt Lopez
Christina Howton*	Mel Fowle
Christine Hill	Mike Herman
Christine Lattanzio	Miriam Gurza*
Christopher J. Potter*	Nadja Ibrahim*
Cynthia Chandler	Naveli Thomas
Daniel Cadoret*	Nicholas Mitchell
Daniel D'Archivio*	Philippe Thieren*
Daniel Peritz*	Rachel Klein
David Baldwin	Rajveer Hundal*
David Baranick	Raymond J. Beier
David Glicksman	Renee Sarria
David Khan*	Rich Fournier
David M. Voss	Rick Barnay*
David Ross	Rob Sciaudone
David Seaman	Ron Bidulka*
David Yee	Ron Walsh*
Deborah Dumoulin*	Russell Sugar*
Dennis Goginsky	Ryan Dumais
Dillon Long	Scott Tornberg
Dominique Fortier*	Scott Williamson
Doug Purdie*	Sean Hiebert*
Douglas B. Struckman	Sergio Lozano
Emily Pillars	Stacie Benes
Eric Andrew*	Stephan Gianoplus
Eric St-Amour*	Stephen Cairns
Ernie Hudson	Steve Baker
Eugene Chan	Steve Hollinger*
Frank Magliocco*	Steve Tyler
Franklin Yanofsky	Steven Weisenburger
Fred Cassano*	Susan Smith
Ian Gunn*	Tim Conlon
Ian T. Nelson	Tori H. Lambert
Jack Keating	Warren Marr
Jackie Yau*	William Hux
Jacqueline Kinneary	William Keating
James Oswald	
Jane Ma*	
Jasen Kwong	*Canada-based.
Jason Chessler	
Jay Schwartz	www.pwc.com/structure

Notice to Readers

Emerging Trends in Real Estate® is a trends and forecast publication now in its 36th edition, and is one of the most highly regarded and widely read forecast reports in the real estate industry. *Emerging Trends in Real Estate® 2015*, undertaken jointly by PwC and the Urban Land Institute, provides an outlook on real estate investment and development trends, real estate finance and capital markets, property sectors, metropolitan areas, and other real estate issues throughout the United States and Canada.

Emerging Trends in Real Estate® 2015 reflects the views of more than 1,400 individuals who completed surveys or were interviewed as a part of the research process for this report. The views expressed herein, including all comments appearing in quotes, are obtained exclusively from these surveys and interviews and do not express the opinions of either PwC or ULI. Interviewees and survey participants represent a wide range of industry experts, including investors, fund managers, developers, property companies, lenders, brokers, advisers, and consultants. ULI and PwC researchers personally interviewed more than 391 individuals, and survey responses were received from 1,055 individuals, whose company affiliations are broken down below.

Private property company investor, or developer	29.3%
Real estate service firm	20.8%
Institutional/equity investor or investment manager	13.3%
Commercial/institutional real estate developer	9.2%
Bank, lender, or securitized lender	8.7%
Publicly listed property company or equity REIT	6.1%
Private REIT or nontraded property company	2.9%
Homebuilder or residential land developer	7.0%
Mortgage REIT or real estate debt investor	1.2%
Other	1.5%

Throughout the publication, the views of interviewees and/or survey respondents have been presented as direct quotations from the participant without attribution to any particular participant. A list of the interview participants in this year's study who chose to be identified appears at the end of this report, but it should be noted that all interviewees are given the option to remain anonymous regarding their participation. In several cases, quotes contained herein were obtained from interviewees who are not listed. Readers are cautioned not to attempt to attribute any quote to a specific individual or company.

PricewaterhouseCoopers has exercised reasonable care in the collecting, processing, and reporting of this information but has not independently verified, validated, or audited the data to verify the accuracy or completeness of the information. PricewaterhouseCoopers gives no express or implied warranties, including but not limited to any warranties of merchantability or fitness for a particular purpose or use and shall not be liable to any entity or person using this document, or have any liability with respect to this document.

To all who helped, the Urban Land Institute and PwC extend sincere thanks for sharing valuable time and expertise. Without the involvement of these many individuals, this report would not have been possible.

Sustaining Momentum but Taking Nothing for Granted

"It is possible to stretch for opportunities—you just have to be aware of how much runway you have left in the current cycle."

Another year, another look at the *Emerging Trends* expected to affect real estate in the coming year and beyond. It's a healthy discipline for our industry, taking a periodic look ahead to evaluate the contenders and pretenders among the forces shaping the real estate business. By survey, by interview, by a review of data, and by a thoughtful sifting through of fact and opinion to arrive at considered judgments, nothing is taken for granted. Each prospective "trend" has to prove itself to a cross section of the industry if it is to make the list.

For 2015, we propose ten top trends for your attention. What are their salient characteristics?

Since real estate's value is a function of how it serves its users—workers, consumers, businesses, travelers, homeowners, and

Exhibit 1-2 **Emerging Trends Barometer 2015**

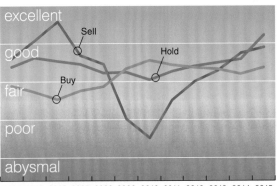

Source: *Emerging Trends in Real Estate* surveys.
Note: Based on U.S. respondents only.

apartment renters—we look to human elements for signs of trends. Demographics, labor force characteristics, location preferences, and motivations discerned by observed behaviors and the interpretation of real estate professionals are among the most reliable indicators of trends.

The physical attributes of the built environment also count. Interviewees consider how properties either enhance or detract from productivity. They worry about obsolescence in the face of change. They care about physical supports such as transportation infrastructure, the power and communications grids, and, in a significant part of the nation, water. None of those issues has emerged overnight; none of them will go away soon. Tackling them effectively can enhance the property markets. Ignoring such issues threatens the economy generally and the property markets in particular.

Exhibit 1-1 **U.S. Real Estate Returns and Economic Growth**

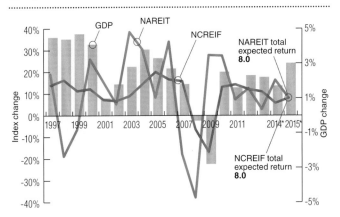

Sources: NCREIF Fund Index Open-End Diversified Core Equity (NFI-ODCE); NAREIT Equity REIT Index; Bureau of Economic Analysis/U.S. Department of Commerce; *World Economic Outlook*, July 2014; *Emerging Trends in Real Estate 2015* survey.

*GDP forecasts are from *World Economic Outlook*; NCREIF/NAREIT data for 2014 are as of second-quarter 2014; 2015 forecasts are based on the *Emerging Trends in Real Estate 2015* survey.

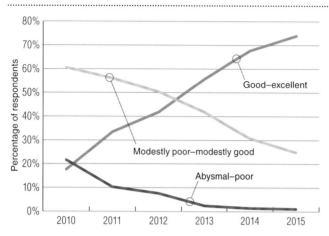

Exhibit 1-3 Firm Profitability Prospects for 2015

(y-axis: Percentage of respondents, 0% to 80%)

Good–excellent

Modestly poor–modestly good

Abysmal–poor

(x-axis: 2010, 2011, 2012, 2013, 2014, 2015)

Source: *Emerging Trends in Real Estate* surveys.
Note: Based on U.S. respondents only.

Financial factors also help define trends, this year and always. The volume and form of our savings as a society count. The flow of capital from around the world influences U.S. real estate mightily. The appetite for risk and the pricing of risk help direct that capital to the preferred geographic locations and property types. Competition hones the pricing of real estate itself, and the various services needed to get the most out of properties. The wide variety of investment opportunities—equity and debt, direct and indirect investment vehicles, the legal structures that offer a range of choices to property professionals—requires us to discuss trends in a specified and nuanced way. Even with a limited number of "top trends," it is important to tell the stories carefully.

With these salient principles in mind, we herewith present our selection of the top trends in real estate for 2015. Let the discussion and debate begin!

1. The 18-Hour City Comes of Age

Twenty years ago, *Emerging Trends* identified the distinction between nine-to-five downtown markets and 24-hour urban markets as the key to superior investment performance. That has proved to be exceptionally prescient, as shown by capital flows, occupancy rates, and relative pricing changes since then. The "24-hour city" concept has become part of the common lexicon of the real estate industry and of city planners.

That trend is expanding and looks to be increasing in influence. No longer is it accepted that only the great coastal cities can be alive around the clock and on weekends. Downtown transformations have combined the key ingredients of housing, retail, dining, and walk-to-work offices to regenerate

urban cores, spurring investment and development and raising the quality of life for a roster of cities. So let's call these reemergent downtowns "18-hour markets." Though they quiet down noticeably in the wee hours, deep into the evening the mix of shops, restaurants, and entertainment truly generates excitement. This is catalyzed by walk-to-work housing that encourages employers in the knowledge and talent industries to keep their offices downtown.

The 18-hour city is emerging across the country. A Nashville developer, for instance, notes that "national players are coming in, drawn by our job growth. The urban core is competing again." "Under the radar, downtowns like Greenville and Charleston have become diverse, following the 24-hour model," says a prominent Southeast broker. "They are alive in the evenings."

Take a look at our 2015 *Emerging Trends* rankings:

- Raleigh-Durham, Charlotte, and Denver are newly placed in the top ten overall scores.

- Charlotte is rated in the top ten for investment—as is Brooklyn, New York. And, they are also listed as best places for development in 2015.

- With homebuilding coming back, at long last, we find Charlotte, Raleigh-Durham, and Denver joined by Portland and Atlanta among the ten most promising markets.

What do most of these 18-hour markets have in common? An ambition expressed in tangible efforts to strengthen their centers as live/work/play environments.

Seeing is believing, and belief in the value proposition for markets getting out of the nine-to-five doldrums has taken root. The trending cities are not Manhattan, and probably don't want to be. But that is their polestar, the model that has demonstrated that the right urban mix bolsters occupancy, that density raises values, and that vibrancy attracts investment capital.

Investing requires a deep knowledge of these local markets. Buyers have more markets to consider now that the 18-hour centers are putting the elements in place to ratchet up their investment capital flows.

2. The Changing Age Game

The millennials are an even bigger cohort—and still growing through immigration—than the baby-boom generation, which has been shaping U.S. economic geography, marketing, consumption, and real estate use since the 1950s. The millennials

Exhibit 1-4 **Real Estate Business Prospects**

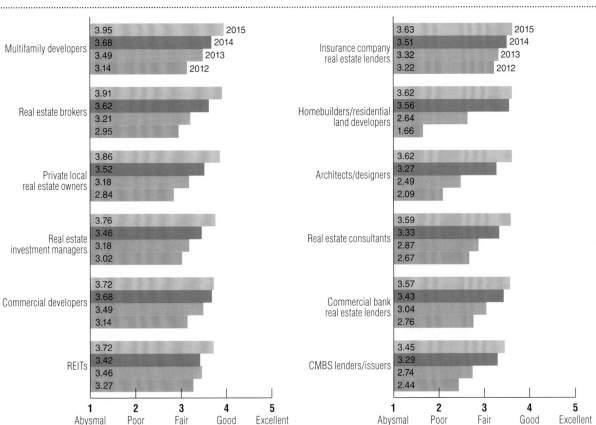

	2015	2014	2013	2012
Multifamily developers	3.95	3.68	3.49	3.14
Real estate brokers	3.91	3.62	3.21	2.95
Private local real estate owners	3.86	3.52	3.18	2.84
Real estate investment managers	3.76	3.46	3.18	3.02
Commercial developers	3.72	3.68	3.49	3.14
REITs	3.72	3.42	3.46	3.27
Insurance company real estate lenders	3.63	3.51	3.32	3.22
Homebuilders/residential land developers	3.62	3.56	2.64	1.66
Architects/designers	3.62	3.27	2.49	2.09
Real estate consultants	3.59	3.33	2.87	2.67
Commercial bank real estate lenders	3.57	3.43	3.04	2.76
CMBS lenders/issuers	3.45	3.29	2.74	2.44

1 Abysmal 2 Poor 3 Fair 4 Good 5 Excellent

Source: *Emerging Trends in Real Estate* surveys.

Notes: Based on U.S. respondents only. Before the 2015 survey, "Commercial developers"' and "Multifamily developers" were combined under the category "Commercial/multifamily developers."

have been much talked about, but for all their impact thus far, there is much more to come. And the changes will accelerate and become more complex over the next ten years.

An institutional investor notes, "Renter-by-choice is still a potent force. Apartments will retain their appeal for a while for millennials, spooked by what happened to homeowning parents." Over time, of course, homeownership will increase as the millennials age. A number of interviewees agree that "investors should be thinking about what millennials will look like in six to seven years." A horizon into the 2020s was cited several times: "Watch for a seven-year trend before millennials will have to make the decision about whether to stay urban or move to outer areas or the suburbs." Condos can enter the picture as well.

Economically, "Millennials have to feel the pressure as $1 trillion in student debt needs to be paid off." A lot will depend upon improved income mobility, since most "millennials are only getting average jobs and they do not have the means to own a

home." Investors do not have to plan on this remaining constant since emerging trends take time to unfold. "A typical investment hold period for a core investment fund is ten years. What will the impact of the millennials be then?"

A healthy amount of disagreement exists about what will happen. One camp is convinced that the millennials will revert to the mean and want private offices and will move to the suburbs to raise families. The other side feels like they will continue with the same behavior they have exhibited. But the key is that we are talking about a large generational cohort that will evolve and segment over time. Painting them with too broad a brush will lead to misplaced expectations—as it has with the baby boomers. One size will not fit all millennials.

The 77 million–strong generation of boomers has not gone out to pasture, even though its leading edge has now reached the putative retirement age. A decade or two ago, the expectation was that resort and retirement communities, mostly in the

Exhibit 1-5 2015 U.S. Population by Age

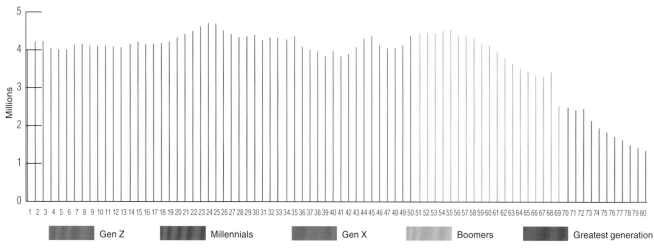

Source: U.S. Census Bureau.

Sunbelt, were going to be the "hot property types" just about now. The *Emerging Trends* survey this year, however, ranked such property as the least desirable investment and development opportunities.

"Aging baby boomers will continue to set trends," said one investor with an international fund. "The leading edge is now 65 to 73 years old. The move to city centers by this group may have more staying power than the millennial generation." As the boomers trend away from stereotypical golf-course retirement, they are creating multiple markets that are "inch deep, not mile deep." Our interviewees considered opportunities in health care properties and seniors' housing "oversold," and underscore the desire of retiring boomers "to own properties near their children." It must be said, though, that under the influence of the Affordable Care Act, new approaches to urgent care, and the repurposing of retail properties both in the suburbs and in the center cities, medical office use can be identified as a strengthening trend for 2015 and the years ahead.

With better health, longer life spans, and net worth that is still seeking to recover from the battering it experienced during the Great Recession, boomers are staying in the workforce—to some degree at the expense of the millennials, notes one interviewee. As that trend wanes, look for increasing income mobility potentially reinvigorating the middle class. As the boomers eventually do retire in greater numbers, "think Carolinas rather than Florida," says one investor.

So, with all the deserved attention being lavished on millennials, let's not ignore the boomers. They will be influencing the market both as workers and retirees for a couple of decades to come. In fact, it is the combined impact of the millennials and the boomers—all 160 million people in the two cohorts—that is making demography such a hugely powerful driving trend right now.

And while we're at it, let's not forget the smaller "generation Z" that is coming along next. Planning for a nation with lesser household formation, fewer new consumers, and a really meager number of workforce entrants is the challenge ahead for a real estate industry with its eye on the 2020s.

3. Labor Markets Are Trending toward a Tipping Point

Raise your hand if you are thinking about a coming shortage of workers. Not skilled workers—that's already here. Those seeking specialists to write computer code are already scanning the continents for those who can produce customized programs and business apps. Forward-looking businesses are waking up to a realization that while we were worried about the "jobless recovery," longer-term labor market trends were moving in exactly the opposite direction. Retirements will accelerate, while the peak of millennial labor force entrants has already passed. Within a few years the talk will be about labor shortages, not labor surpluses. That trend reshapes things in remarkable ways. The notion that "jobs are chasing people" will morph into a primary rule of the labor market. What now applies particularly to people with talent, knowledge, and skill will soon become a widening search

Exhibit 1-6 U.S. Labor Force Growth

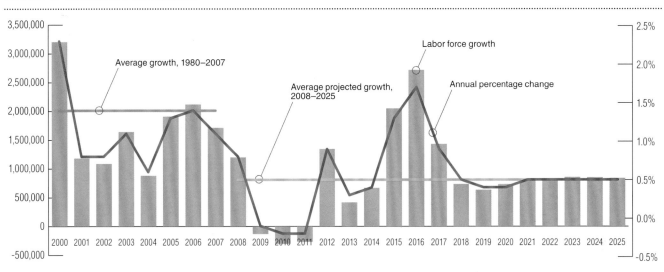

Sources: U.S. Bureau of Labor Statistics; Moody's Analytics (Economic & Consumer Credit Analytics) forecast.

for workers across the entire occupational spectrum. A global search for talent is underway, and the United States needs to prepare for that. The steps need to start immediately.

Survey respondents place job growth at the top of the list of most important issues for real estate, closely followed by the related concerns of wage and income growth. A leading economic consultant says, "Labor force growth in the next few years will drop to the slowest growth rate since the end of WWI

and the influenza breakout. Without a change in immigration policy, the U.S. will face a severe shortage of workers." (Yes, you read that right: "since the end of World War ONE.") Some developers in the Southwest are already reporting feeling the pinch. And what about the disincentives in our visa system? Both the E-5 "investor immigrant" program's constraints and a student visa program that educates international students and then sends them home to compete against the United States are considered ripe for change by our interviewees.

Exhibit 1-7 Potential Skills Gap by Market

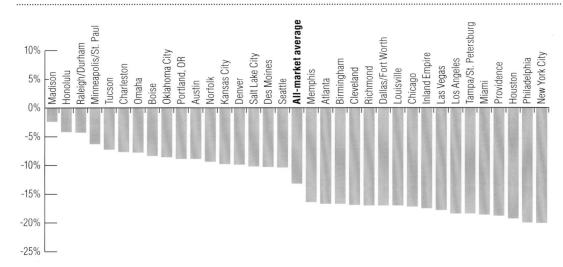

Notes: "Skills gap" is the difference between percentage of job openings projected to require some college and percentage of population with some college. Estimates are for year-end 2012.

Source: Brookings Institution.

Exhibit 1-8 Importance of Issues for Real Estate in 2015

1		3	4	5
No importance		Moderate importance	Considerable importance	Great importance

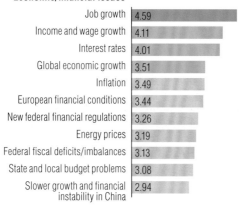

Economic/financial issues

Job growth	4.59
Income and wage growth	4.11
Interest rates	4.01
Global economic growth	3.51
Inflation	3.49
European financial conditions	3.44
New federal financial regulations	3.26
Energy prices	3.19
Federal fiscal deficits/imbalances	3.13
State and local budget problems	3.08
Slower growth and financial instability in China	2.94

Social/political issues

Terrorism/war	3.53
Political gridlock	3.37
Federal government actions	3.35
Lack of qualified workers	3.31
Immigration	3.14
Rising cost of education	2.97
Social equity/inequality	2.75

Real estate/development issues

Construction costs	4.05
Land costs	3.90
Vacancy rates	3.76
Infrastructure funding/development	3.72
Refinancing	3.55
Transportation funding	3.47
Future home prices	3.24
CMBS market recovery	3.20
NIMBYism	3.15
Affordable/workforce housing	3.13
Deleveraging	3.02
Wellness/health features in buildings	2.74
Green buildings	2.67
Risks from extreme weather	2.51

Source: *Emerging Trends in Real Estate 2015* surveys.
Note: Based on U.S. respondents only.

What's the emerging trend? Look for a change in the terms of debate from "defend our borders" to "send us workers" in the coming years.

Is this some radical reaction to U.S. Homeland Security excesses? Not really. Of all groups, the Conference Board—no one's idea of a fringe organization—is the one sounding the alarm about the potential for 15 years of labor scarcity ahead. Its report, *From a Buyers' to a Sellers' Market: Declining Unemployment and Evolving Labor Shortages in the U.S.*, released in May 2014, makes the following points.

- Many of the millions of long-term unemployed are now permanently out of the labor market, either because of skill erosion, age, or being effectively retired. Though these factors weigh on society in many ways, their impact on labor force participation is likely to persist. How many people are we talking about? The most recent Bureau of Labor Statistics figures say that 3.5 million people looking for work have been out of a job for six months or more, in an economy that has been growing by more than 200,000 per month in 2014.

- Data suggest that this is not just a shortage of high-tech or knowledge workers. Truck drivers and health services jobs are seeking qualified applicants. National data in the manufacturing sector show more job openings than new hires since January 2012.

- The voluntary quit rate and employers' reports of skills mismatches are on the rise. We have not yet seen upward wage trends to compensate for the emerging labor shortage. Productivity growth is not making up the difference, either.

Since a profit multiplier is built into labor costs, if firms are to grow their bottom line they will need to bid for labor more aggressively in short order.

What does this mean for real estate? Well, most industry veterans would confirm that job growth is the key factor for filling office buildings and new housing, as well as the driver for improving sales at shopping centers and spending at hotels and resorts. Can real estate prosper during times of low unemployment? Of course! But constraining labor force growth by restrictive immigration policy is counterproductive, notes the Conference Board. The Real Estate Roundtable has joined in with support of a reformed E-5 visa program, while arguing that a cap of 15,000 on lower-wage "W" laborers hobbles the industry's construction recovery.

While those looking at the rearview mirror continue to belabor the claim that the official unemployment rate understates slackness in the job market, the emerging trends are moving in the opposite direction.

4. Real Estate's Love/Hate Relationship with Technology Intensifies

Not a single form of real estate is exempt from the exponential expansion of technology. In an age of digital maturity, interviewees see tech as providing new business tools and environments, opening new business paths, and cycling forward as a source of user demand in an era when more traditional industries may be sluggish. Technology, disruptive and incremental, is pushing change in space use, locations, and demand levels at an accelerated pace. It is now the norm to anticipate, strategize, and respond to new technologies before they are mainstream.

Investors use the presence of tech firms and science, technology, engineering, and math (STEM) workers in a metro area as a screen for acquisition strategies. As we go through a period when financial firms no longer drive office demand, brokers are concentrating on the technology and media industries as a key source of leasing. Retailers look to the internet both as a source of competition and as a way to drive consumers into stores. Warehousing looks different in a world where inventory control reduces store sizes, but demand for same-day fulfillment makes "the last mile" in the supplier-to-consumer chain all the more critical. And so it goes.

As a major Manhattan developer put it, "Demand for office facilities in NYC is strong. The finance sector may be down, but technology and media companies are filling the gap nicely." In consonance with millennial preferences, the tech sector, which was once mostly suburban—Westchester and Dutchess counties in New York; Route 128 in Boston; Silicon Valley; Redmond, Washington; the cadre of firms in Raleigh-Durham's Research Triangle Park—is now more urban. Think of the impact that tech companies are having in Manhattan and Chicago, as well as in the Bay Area.

One pension fund fiduciary believes that "downsizing of office and retail will continue as technology enhances workability, shopping, and overall living." Still, some think it inadvisable to assume we know the end results of current changes. In the words of one insurance company executive, "We observe the impact of technology on all sectors, but we don't know how much space will be needed over time for office, warehouse, [and] retail. The consequences probably won't be as dramatic as some might fear."

The rise of the sharing economy, finding success with the millennial generation, which is very comfortable sharing rather than owning, is already having a disruptive effect on the taxi and hotel industries. The office property type, particularly the segment serving smaller tenants, could be turned upside down by the advent of landlords offering collaborative and shared-office locations, as well as lessees renting out unused conference rooms by the hour or a day of office space. This, in fact, is already a fairly familiar business model both in office incubators and in the business suites business. The question is, "Will this go viral?" Tenants have the ability to adjust their space to meet their current economic needs. For example, if a firm is in product development and has 15 employees, it might need 2,500 to 3,000 square feet of office space; then, when the product is ready for market, they are using ten marketing employees who are in the office only part-time. Their space needs decline to 1,000 to 1,500 square feet. No need to sign a lease locking you into 3,000 square feet—the firm can adjust its needs based on what it needs. In addition, the firm has the freedom to offer its excess space to another firm. This type of leasing model could have a significant impact on how smaller office spaces are leased.

Visionaries in the industry think that we'll see trends developing whereby accelerated obsolescence will be routinely factored into property decisions. A chief executive officer (CEO) of a Southeast real estate services firm believes that "amortization of improvements will assume greater importance." He goes on to ask, "What does a world of driverless cars and drone deliveries mean for the acres of parking lots surrounding shopping malls? What happens to real estate brokerage in a world of big data?"

Overall, the fear factor about technological disruption is easing, with only a very moderate 2.7 score on the "issues impacting your business decisions" survey question. E-commerce, for example, is being viewed as an adaptation challenge, as retailers become "omnichannel distributors" and e-tailers begin to open brick-and-mortar stores. The trend? Anticipation and evolution, and only the adaptive survive. The initial winners? Logistics firms at the intersection of wholesale and retail trade.

5. Event Risk Is Here to Stay

There is nothing new in seeing investors along the continuum from "core" to "opportunistic." That's now classic. But the trend will be that such distinctions are heightened over time, and 2015 looks to be a year when this will be especially evident. But why?

Because we see concern about "event risk" troubling the minds of more and more interviewees. Geopolitical risks multiplied in number and intensity in 2014 and threaten to cascade further, and that has pushed the "flight to safety" in global capital to the fore. If you think U.S. Treasury rates are low, in early September two-year yields on European sovereign debt turned negative. In effect, investors were paying banks to hold their money for

Exhibit 1-9 **World Regions Targeted, by Investor Location**

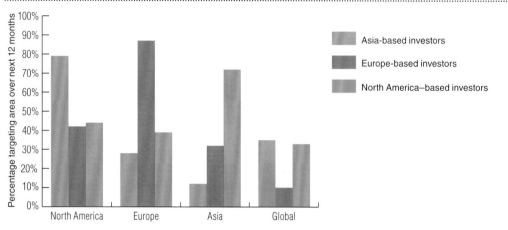

Source: Prequin.

them. That's "risk off" to an extreme. Little wonder, then, that international investors are considered to be the best prospect for increasing investment volume in 2015, according to the *Emerging Trends* survey.

The propensity for offshore wealth to find a home—literally—in the United States is a condition of long standing. Latin American families have flocked to the Miami area for many years. Luxury units in the New York area have long been a part of that city's cosmopolitan flavor. But now, sovereign wealth funds, old family money, and high-net-worth individuals enjoying initial public offering (IPO) proceeds are all converging on the United States for investment opportunities. Real estate in all its forms has great appeal as a durable, proven asset class in a risky world.

Today's offshore capital inflow is different in kind, as well as in degree. International investment in U.S. real estate is spread across dozens of markets, and all income-producing property types. In the 12 months ending July 31, 2014, $50.3 billion in globally sourced capital acquired U.S. real property. The Canadians represented the lion's share, at $15.1 billion. But a veritable "spanning the world" lineup each put between $2 billion and $4 billion to work: Norway, China, Japan, Hong Kong, Germany, Israel, and Australia all were in that league. And that's the most obvious of the flows. Many international investors use commingled funds or invest through tax havens like Bermuda.

By and large, foreign capital remains concentrated on the usual suspects: the gateway cities. The Sunbelt is making something of a comeback, attracting offshore capital to Phoenix ($700 million) and the Texas markets (Houston, $1.1 billion, and Dallas, $1 billion) for apartments, and Hawaii ($2 billion) and south Florida ($1.1 billion) for hotels. Development capital, especially

from China, is making an impact in Los Angeles, Las Vegas, and Miami, as well as in New York's burgeoning outer-borough market, Brooklyn. In a sense, the recent propensity of offshore investors to expand their roster of investment preferences is another sign of risk management—spreading their interests across a wider geography is a way to limit downside volatility in any one place.

Yield-oriented investors aren't ceding the field. Value-add and opportunistic investments are considered to have the best prospects for 2015 returns, according survey respondents, although they think good, high-quality deals are difficult to find. But the best indicator that both conservative and aggressive investors will do well in 2015's environment is the expectation that National Council of Real Estate Investment Fiduciaries (NCREIF) and National Association of Real Estate Investment Trusts (NAREIT) returns will rise 60 to 90 basis points by 2020. Increasing returns over time portend increasing capital flows, a trend that is good across the board for the industry.

Bottom line: America's diversity—*heterogeneity*, to use academics' current buzzword—is a strength and a shield. It is a strength because in a world of dire risk, it gives both domestic and international capital a chance not only to park money, but also to find markets and real estate opportunities that match a whole range of preferences. It is a shield because the dense web of the U.S. economy makes for greater resilience when shocks occur.

This year, *Emerging Trends* interviewees were sensitive to potential "black swan" developments. "It isn't what you see, it is what you don't see," as one economic forecaster put it. Accommodating the potential for a downturn almost defines the

Exhibit 1-10 Investment Prospects by Asset Class

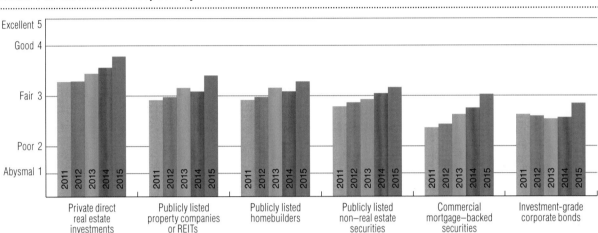

Source: *Emerging Trends in Real Estate* surveys.

Note: Based on U.S. respondents only.

essence of responsible management. While hunkering down for an apocalypse is not a widespread strategy, and certainly not a trend, a concern for capital conservation is clearly abroad in the marketplace. That is most likely a trend that will have legs as long as the world remains unduly exposed to the black swan of event risk.

6. A Darwinian Market Keeps the Squeeze on Companies

Competition is unrelenting, and the need to have a clear "brand identity" is important as firms seek to navigate in the swift stream of capital. For those in the public markets, dependent upon the understanding of Wall Street analysts, the more "pure play" the better. Hence, the recent spin-off activities in the retail, office, and hospitality real estate investment trust (REIT) sectors sound a theme that will echo as a trend in 2015. One analyst notes that while "industry metrics are good, it is hard to be accretive merely through acquisitions. Companies need to sharpen their focus." Some see this as a necessary discipline, a sign of maturity for the industry, and a harbinger of greater stability ahead. The drive for efficiency and effectiveness in both service delivery and cost will filter from investor expectations down to the service providers.

That applies on the institutional investment side as well, leading one public pension plan sponsor to say that "replacing under-performing investment managers" should be expected going forward. Pension funds are looking to go more direct or "hands-

on." The largest investors seek more control. This reduces the number of new managers you might have seen at this point in the real estate cycle, according to an industry association officer. A few niche managers are offering funds. Capital raising is difficult for mid-tier managers.

One upshot: fees (again) are going to be squeezed as the capital sources want more services for less money. After a long period in which outsourcing was the fundamental approach (staying "lean and mean"), there is some indication that bringing real estate talent in-house is not only an improvement in accountability, but also more cost-effective. Though this is going on in just a slice of the industry, consolidation could accelerate as this trend gathers momentum.

Meanwhile, capital raising in Europe has gotten more difficult with the Alternative Investment Fund Managers Directive (AIFMD). New regulations vastly increase reporting and compliance requirements. Some managers will just not be able to afford operating under AIFMD, reducing the number of private equity firms and hedge funds sourcing capital from the European Union, in the view of one such investor.

As more and more capital has become available, more and more players naturally have been looking to tap the cash. That leads to overpopulation in the field. Look for a winnowing-out process as the next step. The brokerage industry, it might be noted, is already well advanced in this process. Other business lines will be moving down that path.

Exhibit 1-11 401(k) Asset Allocation by Participant Age

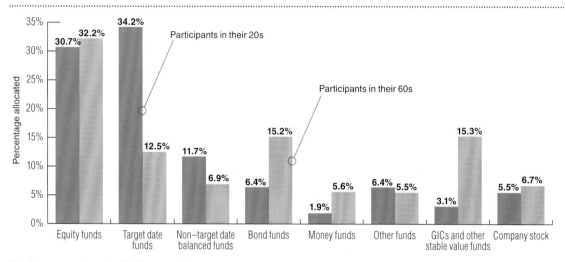

Note: Average asset allocation of 401(k) account balances, year-end 2012. Funds include mutual funds, bank collective trusts, life insurance separate accounts, and any pooled investment product primarily invested in the security indicated. Percentages are dollar-weighted averages. Components do not add up to 100 percent because of rounding.

Source: Investment Company Institute.

7. A New 900-Pound Gorilla Swings into View

Emerging Trends 2014 alerted readers to the establishment of the Defined Contribution Real Estate Council, formed "to help plan sponsors and their participants achieve better investment outcomes through the use of institutional quality real estate." U.S. retirement assets hit $23 trillion in 2014, and more than half of that was in defined contribution (DC) or individual retirement account (IRA) funds. As one interviewee put it, "We will be seeing retirees become their own chief investment officers."

How deep is this pool of funds? According to the Investment Company Institute, there are $6.6 trillion in IRAs and $6.0 trillion in DC 401(k) plans as of the first quarter of 2014. Compare this with the remaining $3.0 trillion in corporate defined-benefit pension plans and the $5.4 trillion in public sector pension funds. An institutional-like allocation of 5 percent to real estate would represent $300 billion of DC 401(k) funds alone.

Exhibit 1-12 U.S. Retirement Assets

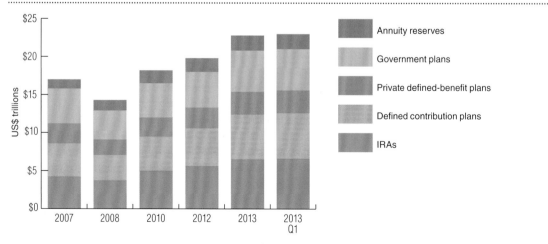

Source: Investment Company Institute, *Research and Statistics Report*, June 25, 2014.

Who can doubt that new products directed specifically to this capital source will be emerging over the coming years? As one interviewee put it, the real estate industry is challenged "to create a better option for this generation." This may mean needing to educate the army of certified financial analysts (CFAs) about commercial property.

Even at a modest allocation level, we are talking about hundreds of billions of dollars of potential real estate capital. It has implications for pricing, certainly, but also should prompt a round of serious thinking about fiduciary responsibility in managing this money. Retirees are absolutely "capital conservation" oriented, and the immediate time horizon for asset-liability duration is far different from the long-term hold consideration of the established defined-benefit managers. Liquidity is especially important, and this may favor REITs as a vehicle over direct investments. CFAs, versed in stocks and bonds, may like the REITs as an entry point into the commercial property arena.

Whether in securitized or direct property investment, though, there will be a learning curve that will include (at some point) the painful lesson that real estate can go down as well as up. But with a combined $12.6 trillion in capital, IRAs and DC funds absolutely will be identifying and taking advantage of the benefits of having high-quality commercial property in a mixed-asset portfolio.

Watch this trend. It could be huge.

8. Infrastructure: Time for the United States to Get Serious?

If you were to play a word association game, what word would you pair with the term *infrastructure*? *Aging, crumbling, decrepit, failing*? Now well into the 21st century, we rely upon roads, bridges, transit, water systems, an electric grid, and a communications network put in place 50, 75, even 100 or more years ago. It is largely hidden and taken for granted—until it stops working. Then you can't get to work, power up your computer, or even take a shower.

As more and more Americans travel abroad, they wonder why we can't have roads like the Autobahn, trains like the Eurostar TVG, or cellphone reception as clear as that available on the Great Wall of China. The American Society of Civil Engineers (ASCE) gives U.S. infrastructure a grade of D+ on its most recent report card.

For all our vaunted technological innovations, the foundation of our commerce is eroding around us. Sadly, it is not just bridges,

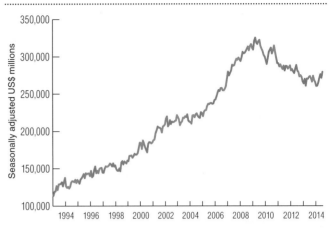

Exhibit 1-13 **Total Public Construction Spending**

Source: U.S. Federal Reserve.

roads, and the like (as important as they are). Since 2009, spending on educational buildings and health care facilities—by both the public and private sectors—is down by one-third in real-dollar terms. As a nation, the United States is not investing in the physical facilities needed to compete into the future. The trend here is not good, and it is going to be painful for real estate if problems are left to worsen.

An investor with deep experience in logistics believes that congestion is not just a goods-movement problem. "Infrastructure constraints causing congestion hobble the improvements technology can provide. The millennial generation is intolerant of congestion and delay—on highways and in transit." If the pursuit of the millennials is central to your city's economic development or your firm's business strategy, that's alarming. A top New York broker laments, "Real estate depends upon ease of commutation. Businesses are paying close attention to commutation patterns of employees, realizing that the people you most want are also the most 'footloose' as employees. Fundamentally, all businesses need talent [and customers], and you 'solve back' to the real estate from that."

The chief investment officer of a public retirement fund wants to invest in growth markets. But he expects "less growth in areas not investing in infrastructure." A private equity firm with holdings concentrated in the Boston–Washington corridor comments, "Infill is the key to opportunity in strong markets, but it is a challenge when transportation and utility infrastructure is old and seriously underfunded."

Out West—beyond the 100th meridian particularly—the future depends desperately on water. The 14-year drought in the Colorado River basin has brought Lake Mead to its lowest level since the Hoover Dam was constructed during the Great Depression. The level of the lake has dropped 100 feet during this drought, and 150 feet from its high water mark in 1983. This has cities like Denver, Phoenix, Las Vegas, and Los Angeles scrambling, and has the federal government initiating a pilot program to pay cash as an incentive to reduce water use. Needless to say, if these cities were to face serious growth constraints on population gains because of water deficiency, that would alter America's real estate map considerably. A valuation specialist with a national practice had this to say: "How do we get what we need where we need it?" Droughts have been coming more frequently and are longer lasting. Can we figure out the transportation of water? Pipelines, easements, pricing?

Some light at the end of the tunnel may come from the increasing tendency of public agencies to turn to public/private partnerships (PPPs) as the vehicle for addressing the infrastructure crisis. The daunting price tag of needed improvements, coupled with the straitjackets constraining public budgets, has prompted a wider degree of cooperation. The PPP approach is not a panacea, of course. The private sector needs to earn a return, and public agencies face political pressure if the return is derived from increased user fees (with tax increases not even on the table in most places). It is a conundrum.

On this subject, we are behind the curve already. ASCE estimates that the needed repair programs for existing, identified infrastructure needs will cost $2.2 trillion over the next five years. Yet, a funding proposal for $50 billion to $75 billion and the enabling legislation to create a national infrastructure bank are mired in Washington politics. Unfortunately, the trend of infrastructure quality and reliability is negative, both in the immediate and in the mid-range future. It may take a catastrophe to move us off this particular dime.

9. Housing Steps Off the Roller Coaster

There were numerous reasons to be aghast at the housing fiasco and the vast amount of collateral damage that was inflicted on the economy and the financial system. Prior to the bubble, housing itself was thought to be "too big to fail." Not only was the value total for residential real estate huge—in excess of $20 trillion—but it was so granular that few economists believed it vulnerable to systemic collapse. But collapse it did, leading the nation—and the world—on an epic, stomach-churning roller-coaster ride.

Remarkably, housing seems to be putting the excesses of the bubble and the ensuing collapse behind it. The trend in residential real estate looks to be returning to the classic principles of supply and demand, with great sensitivity to any deviation from equilibrium quickly reflected in transaction volume and pricing. As this major segment of the economy—still the principal repository of wealth for tens of millions of households—returns to textbook fundamentals, we should see increasing confidence emerge in the residential sector. There could hardly be a more positive trend for the economy as a whole.

What undergirds such a hopeful outlook? Even as the housing market became severely dislocated, the growth in the number of U.S. households continued at a steady pace. Rental housing benefited while single-family-home construction plummeted.

Exhibit 1-14 Existing Homes for Sale and Months' Supply

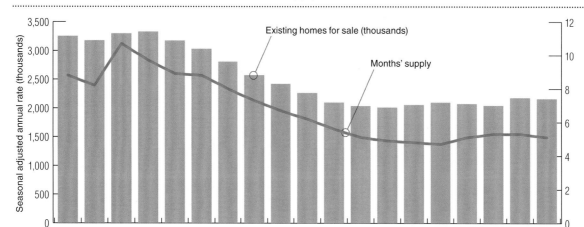

Source: National Association of Realtors.

Exhibit 1-15 Change in Disposable Income, Median Home Sales Price, and Affordability

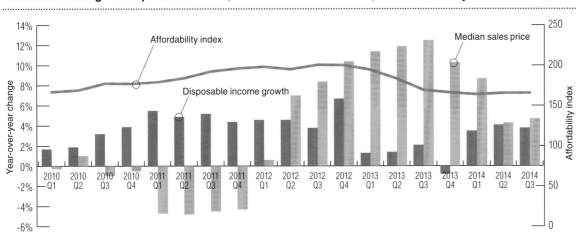

Sources: U.S. Bureau of Economic Analysis; S&P Dow Jones Indices; National Association of Realtors.

The result, over a period of years, has been an enormous shortfall in the supply of new for-sale units. That shortfall now amounts to 9 million homes.

The production shortfall, in turn, has enabled the "months of supply" figure calculated by the National Association of Realtors (NAR) to hover around five months since late 2012, with existing-home sales averaging 2.1 million over the same period. There seems to be a point of balance for single-family residential, and it has stayed steady around that point for two years now. That's a good thing.

Meanwhile, though, disposable income growth for American households has been lagging seriously. Homebuilders—and their lenders—clearly recognize that the recent price recovery in housing has outstripped incomes. And this time there is no funny money being generated in shady mortgage deals. So prices are not reinflating to bubble levels. In other words, discipline looks to be governing the market. Thanks to low interest rates, the NAR's Affordability Index is still relatively high at 165, so the market should enjoy decent liquidity even if rates bump up.

A healthy story is shaping up, whereby housing should anticipate moderate price increases, solidly based on buyers' ability to pay, fluctuating in a fairly narrow band along with minor ups and downs in the NAR's existing-home sales figures. It is a healthy—if boring—story. But after the thrill ride of the past decade in housing, boring is a very, very good trend to report.

10. Keeping an Eye on the Bubble—Emerging Concerns

The generally positive outlook flowing from this year's *Emerging Trends* interviews and survey does have a dark side. Upcycles breed optimism, but excessive optimism can promote reckless-ness. Some interviewees asked, with good reason, whether real estate will soon forget the hard-learned lessons of the recent past. Such prophets of caution are worth listening to, if the respondents to our survey are right. Equity underwriting will be less rigorous in 2015 than in 2014, say 40 percent of the responses across all sources of equity. Easing of standards on the debt side will be even greater, with 42.1 percent seeing lenders loosening next year. And this is happening at a moment when mortgage spreads are already tight, and Treasury rates will inevitably rise.

Exhibit 1-16 Time Horizon for Investing

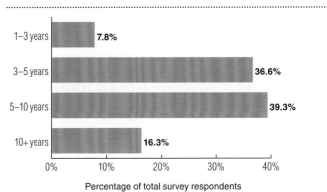

Percentage of total survey respondents

Source: *Emerging Trends in Real Estate 2015* surveys.

Note: Based on U.S. respondents only.

Exhibit 1-17 Sales of Large Commercial Properties in the United States

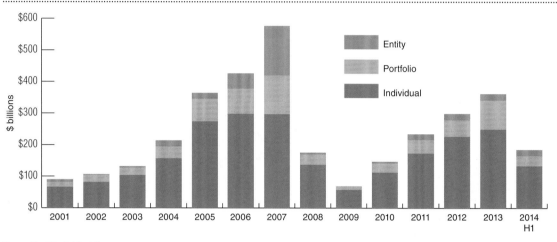

Source: Real Capital Analytics.

Note: Based on independent reports of properties and portfolios valued at $2.5 million and greater. Before 2005, RCA primarily captured sales valued at $5 million and above.

One institutional investor is watching "the little warning signs" of assets priced above replacement cost and the enthusiasm for "Texas markets that are notorious" for boom/bust cycles. A REIT executive calls capital "disciplined for now, but it could become unbridled." A wary West Coast investor urges avoiding the temptation to be "a fly-in investor." Right now, he thinks, acquisitions require "deep market knowledge." Ask the question, "If the local guys won't buy, why should you?"

The sense that recently disciplined capital may be on the verge of becoming too aggressive should give us pause. Emergent trends are vitally important, but carry the danger of being extrapolated into the future. As you read through the body of this year's *Emerging Trends in Real Estate* report, remember that only those who grasp that every trend is of limited duration can stay on the right side of this cyclical industry.

The very gradual nature of the economic recovery carries the risk of lulling the market into some sense of complacency. There has been no big "rebound year" that would typically bring signs of overheating. But our interviewees detected that pricing, underwriting standards, and deal economics have gotten ahead of market fundamentals. The macroeconomics for 2015 are looking favorable, and fundamentals may catch up. Or may not.

"Cyclical risk needs to be watched. This recovery, at five years, is getting too long for comfort. When have we ever had a ten-year upcycle in real estate?" asks a private equity manager. An even more skeptical investment manager worries, "When does the experiment in central banking come to an end? Then we face a major asset bubble event." He sees risk mitigation as the

primary challenge right now, and is mitigating risk by stabilizing all assets in the short run, and deliberately staggering lease and financing terms.

It is healthy to keep such concerns in the conversation. In a period of rising optimism, those warning of potential trouble ahead are sometimes labeled "Cassandras." Here's the thing: those who remember Homer's *Odyssey* recognize Cassandra as the one who warned the Trojans about bringing the Greeks' gift horse into the city. Turns out she was right.

The takeaway emerging trend? For 2015, real estate still benefits from "once-burned, twice-shy" experience. In most cycles, we would have seen overbuilding and excess leverage gathering steam by now. To the degree that hasn't happened, the industry

Exhibit 1-18 Average Length of Economic Cycles, Trough to Trough

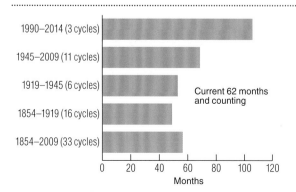

Source: National Bureau of Economic Research.

looks likes it has learned some lessons in self-regulation and self-correction. The balancing of risk and reward is extremely difficult. Celebrate those who are vigilant about overexuberance, but keep an ear out for those warning signs of frothiness. The time to be concerned about bubbles is *before* they burst.

Expected Best Bets for 2015

The following investment and development sentiments from *Emerging Trends* interviewees and survey respondents deserve particular attention in 2015.

1. A Great Time to Be "Seeking Alpha"

Last year, we indicated that active management could "bring success and profits . . . to those with real estate operating and management skills." Market evolution over the last 12 months has elevated that trend to "best bet" level for 2015. Asset selection and market timing may be regarded skeptically by efficient market portfolio theorists. But they are the *raison d'être* for those who make their reputations—and their profits—by outperforming market benchmarks.

Value-add propositions play to real estate's strengths in a rising market cycle, which is the basic playing field for property in 2015. The Blue Chip Economists' consensus forecast calls for above-trend gross domestic product (GDP) growth in late 2014 and throughout 2015. Unemployment is projected to drop to 5.5 percent, and Consumer Price Index (CPI) inflation is predicted to be just above 2 percent. Factor in still-low levels of new commercial construction, and bets on the future look solid.

Class C+ to B properties that can be purchased at cap rates 100 to 200 basis points below the premier assets, and properties upgraded to B+ quality benefit from both improved cash flow as occupancy and rents trend upward, but will enjoy a value bump from cap rates as well. The Grade A properties have been scooped up in the past few years, but the volume of capital in play needs placement. That money will understand and respond to a well-conceived, well-documented value-add story. Not every property will qualify, but those that do are worth a "best bet" call. Look to submarkets near gateway city central business districts (CBDs), mid- to high-rise apartments in transit-served suburbs, and turnaround retail in midsized but growing Sunbelt markets. Deep market knowledge and hands-on skills will be rewarded.

2. Exploit Technology as an Ally of Real Estate, Not Its Enemy

Let's face it—we face an increasingly technological future, and there is no percentage in betting on King Canute trying to hold

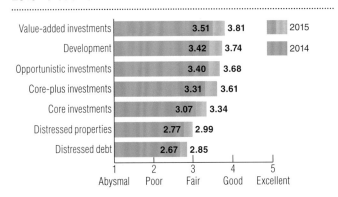

Exhibit 1-19 Prospects by Investment Category/Strategy, 2015 versus 2014

Category	2015	2014
Value-added investments	3.51	3.81
Development	3.42	3.74
Opportunistic investments	3.40	3.68
Core-plus investments	3.31	3.61
Core investments	3.07	3.34
Distressed properties	2.77	2.99
Distressed debt	2.67	2.85

Scale: 1 Abysmal, 2 Poor, 3 Fair, 4 Good, 5 Excellent

Source: *Emerging Trends in Real Estate* surveys.
Note: Based on U.S. respondents only.

back the tide by royal edict. Millennials think of social media as an indispensable tool and want nothing more than the apps that make life easier, more productive, and more fun. That's the trajectory ahead, and real estate companies that can harness the power of social media to manage and market property will gain enormous advantage over laggards in this arena.

Although the technology is "virtual," those using it are very much flesh-and-blood. The densest social networking markets are also the densest physical markets for real estate. That shouldn't be surprising, but it is to many people who have bought the "death of distance" story, the concept that location doesn't matter as much in an electronically connected world. That idea is, in a word, debunked. Entrepreneurship studies, venture capital placement, biotech patents, and real estate values themselves have all now produced impressive evidence that place still matters.

Within those places, though, the ability to communicate swiftly and effectively does not come automatically. Some will invest in the tools and invest in those who know how to use them. Others will be halfhearted in such investment, to their regret. One interesting sign emerging from our interviews: CEOs who are promoting "reverse mentoring," using millennial savvy to educate top managers on just how to get the message out to the millennials. Youth, as they say, must be served.

3. Refinance Now for the Longest Possible Term

The re-fi window has been open for a while now; and with the volume of capital available, it will continue to be open to borrowers. Debt issuance—new lending plus refinancing—is running at a good but not spectacular pace: about $69 billion in commercial mortgage–backed securities (CMBS) by late

September, around $70 billion in commercial mortgages at banks, according to Fed data through late August 2014, and just over $25 billion from American Council of Life Insurers (ACLI) reporting insurance companies. This is not an awful lot of borrowing when placed against the $3.2 trillion size of the commercial real estate debt market in the United States.

While the lending window will stay open, the prices available to borrowers will not remain as favorable as they are today. The yield curve is still relatively flat, and low through the seven- to ten-year maturities that count most for commercial properties. Even with the Fed's assurances, the market fully expects rising rates and a steepening yield curve ahead of us. We are nearing the end of a historic opportunity to lock in long-term mortgage money at exceptionally cheap rates. There should be a real sense of urgency to accomplish this in 2015, early in the year if at all possible.

Those who don't will be muttering "coulda, woulda, shoulda" later in the decade.

4. Develop Industrial

There is a rare confluence of trends favoring industrial properties, and developers in this sector have an exceptional opportunity to capitalize as the trends align. The reshoring of manufacturing, a renewal of homebuilding, the alteration of retailing business models, the reassertion of economic and demographic growth beyond the coastal metro areas, the need for logistical firms to refocus on "last mile" issues as much as on the "hubs" of giant distribution centers—all of these factors point to a need for new industrial space in dozens of markets around the country.

The opportunity has not gone unnoticed by capital providers, as revealed by the comments of this year's *Emerging Trends* interviewees. Existing industrial properties are rated as a solid "buy" in our survey. In 2015, this sector offers a great opportunity for builders, and this looks to be the case through 2017.

5. Don't Give Up on the Suburbs—Differentiate between Good, Bad, and Ugly

Some of our interviewees are pushing back on the enthusiasm for urbanizing markets, calling the concept "oversubscribed." There is indeed a tendency to draw trends in broad strokes, and the back-to-the-city movement is not all that's happening. As capital has disproportionately flowed to highly concentrated locations, a number of suburban markets now appear comparatively inexpensive and yet have "good bones" that will serve them well going forward.

The good: many of the "edge city" locations that combine office, retail, and residential areas effectively—especially those that have two characteristics. Those attributes are sufficient density to support live/work/play interactions, and a combination of transit and walkability. The traditional "railroad suburbs" come to mind, as do small suburban downtowns close to major markets—but so do places like Tempe, where the campus of Arizona State University supports an "18-hour city" energy, and some formerly tired retail malls that have reconfigured themselves as destination mixed-use developments. And don't write off the most dominant traditional malls, even in secondary cities.

Exhibit 1-20 **Inflation and Interest Rate Changes**

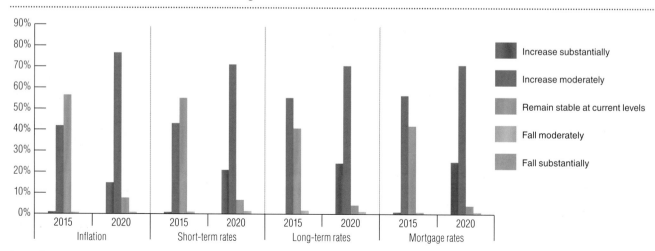

Source: *Emerging Trends in Real Estate 2015* surveys.
Note: Based on U.S. respondents only.

The bad: anything "garden variety." Over the short haul, anyway, there is not much demand from either users or investors for plain-vanilla highway-dependent office parks, or other real estate that falls into the "commodity" bucket. They are cheap, but you get what you pay for.

The ugly: anything that smacks of "sprawl" or of "yesterday's hot concept." If a property is dependent upon an inflated parking ratio, take a pass. If a property is operationally tied to demand that presumes the growth of tract housing at the perimeter of a metro area, run the other way. If you find a property without a cogent appeal to either millennials or baby boomers, time is not on your side.

Some suburbs, in other words, can make the cut as a "best bet," but that's a very select set. Use some commonsense litmus tests to figure out the good, bad, and ugly buckets.

Real Estate Capital Flows

"On the debt side, it is like shooting fish in a barrel."

The tide has come back in. An oceanic flow of capital is surging through America's real estate markets, tugged by gravity and pushed by tailwinds. Rising tides, as the cliché goes, are thought to lift all boats. Yet memories of the last tsunami and the detritus that can still be found littering the landscape from place to place are keeping eyes glued to the weather glass, lest a squall blow in at the high water mark.

The managing director of one institutional investor says, "I expect transaction volumes to be very strong in 2015. Bidding wars are now going on. There is more capital looking to buy than there are opportunities." A West Coast developer thinks that managing director is correct: "The trend of more institutional capital will accelerate." A senior officer with an international developer/owner firm sees this involving more than just the institutions. "There is more capital than there are uses for it," he finds. "Sovereign wealth funds are coming here that haven't been seen before."

So the issue for 2015 is not the volume of liquidity supporting the industry, it is navigation. In every enterprise, a basic need to chart the course exists. That is what virtually all *Emerging Trends* interviewees stressed as their key to success into the future. The prevailing sentiment is the need to maintain rationality, to avoid getting caught up in the flood of capital, being pushed by the tide rather than using it to best advantage. That requires considerable discipline.

One prominent retail property executive stressed that "abundant capital does not equal undisciplined capital for the year or two ahead." He is encouraged that "there is more 'skin in the game' throughout the capital stack, from lower LTVs [loan-to-values] to greater lender reserve requirements." The chief executive officer (CEO) of one untraded real estate investment trust (REIT) acknowledged those conditions, with a caveat: "The market is

very liquid and buoyant. I do not see that changing any time soon. My only concern would be that people are still fairly disciplined . . . at this moment. But the debt side may be on the verge of becoming too aggressive." As Melville's Ishmael prayed in *Moby Dick*, "Oh, Time, Strength, Cash, and Patience!"

That CEO's concern is validated by a look at the risk premium priced into the mortgage rates of the American Council of Life Insurers (ACLI). The chart showing the mortgage rate risk premium is simply the ACLI mortgage constant, across all loans, less the risk-free Treasury note rate. The green horizontal line shows the 65th percentile of such spreads since 1995, while the red line represents the 35th percentile. The area between those lines represents, in some rough fashion, the "normal" spread for

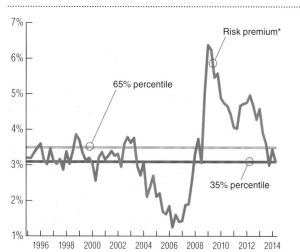

Exhibit 2-1 **Risk Premium in Mortgage Rate**

Sources: The American Council of Life Insurers (ACLI), Federal Reserve, NPV Advisors.
*Risk premium is the ACLI mortgage constant, across all loans, less the seven-year Treasury rate.

mortgage rates. It is clear how insurers kept their spreads disciplined within that normal range from 1995 to 2003, but became excessively aggressive in the "Niagara of capital" years (i.e., 2004–2007). And then, draining liquidity from the market in the de-levering move prompted by the financial crisis, the lenders pushed spreads up so that loan risk was richly priced until 2013. Now it is obvious that "risk on" is the signal, as spreads in the first half of 2014 bumped along toward the bottom of the normal spread range, touching the red line.

Emerging Trends survey respondents, as a group, recognize lenders' increased readiness to accept risk as a condition for putting their money to work. Relatively few believe that debt standards will become more stringent in the coming year. While most foresee lenders carrying over their 2014 underwriting standards in the short run, a substantial minority (about 40 percent) expect less rigorous reviews as loan applications seek to tap an ample pool of debt capital.

Looking across the Debt Sector

A top investment manager based in the Northeast is blunt: "Buyers and lenders are not pricing risk appropriately." A small developer in the Southeast marvels, "On the debt side, it is like shooting fish in a barrel. Whenever we go to market [for a loan], we are choosing between as many people as we ask. For the last few years, we have been financing huge amounts and are locking long." A fund manager at a major institutional investor underscores the point: "The continued loosening of debt underwriting standards will be one of the most important trends in 2015." In the words of a New York–based investment adviser, "This is a great time to be a borrower."

"Risk on" may be appropriate in a putatively rising phase of a cycle. But over the long haul, lenders will not want to be holding long-term paper in an upward-interest-rate climate. It's a good thing that commercial mortgage–backed security (CMBS) volume has been returning, from the perspective of originators and borrowers. But the perspective of those in the last decade's conduit business ("Always remember that you are in the moving, not the storage, business.") didn't turn out to be as savvy as the smart money supposed. Someone is always left holding risky assets that they thought could be unloaded in a timely fashion. Trends can turn with unmerciful suddenness. That is a lesson worth remembering.

Commercial Banks

Commercial banks have substantially finished their deleveraging and the restructuring of their legacy loans. This is especially true of the largest institutions, though regional and local banks

still need to unwind some of their distressed assets. Banking profits have risen, with banking net income at $40.24 billion in the second quarter of 2014, representing the second-highest performance for the sector in the past 23 years. Rising loan volumes and lower loan loss setasides helped banks bolster their bottom lines. Banks see credit quality improving, and increasing volumes are now being driven by business loans, rather than mortgages.

That's still good news for real estate as it enables corporate expansions and may support further hiring, both of which fuel user demand for commercial property. Beyond that indirect benefit, the July 2014 Federal Reserve survey of senior loan officers showed moderately easier mortgage lending standards (though about at the midpoint of their historical level) in the face of rapidly rising borrower demand.

Development has historically leaned on bank financing as its primary source of funds, and this is an area where the trend of rising volume should be apparent in the near and mid-range future. In the Southeast, large regional banks are providing construction funding at 80 percent LTV and 75 percent loan-to-cost, 1.20 debt-service coverage (DSC), 50 percent preleasing requirement, and sponsorship guarantees of 125 percent of partner interests, according to one seasoned Carolinas-based real estate executive. Rates can be locked in as low as 3.9 percent. An officer at a large office REIT identifies banks as the cheapest source of development funding, although they are the toughest on underwriting. *Emerging Trends* survey respondents are about evenly divided between those thinking that development lending requirements will stay stable in 2015 (41.6 percent) and those who feel that lenders will ease their criteria (42.4 percent). Only 16 percent believe that construction lenders will tighten in the coming year.

Investment Banks

Emerging Trends interviewees have their sonar, radar, and GPS on full alert as Wall Street jumps back into real estate lending. It's not as though the money itself is unwelcome. It's just that with ample funds available from so many other sources, and so cheaply, who would want to jump through the hoops entailed in the debt securitization process? With CMBS again ramping up, one interviewee asked, "Will the lid come off the blender again?"

U.S. CMBS volume was $86.1 billion in 2013, and had hit $68.6 billion by late September 2014. So $90 billion for full-year 2014 could be achievable, and an expectation for at least $100 billion 2015 is the conservative consensus. A pension fund investor commented, "We are just sort of cautious about lending practices and how the structures will be reformatted to eliminate the precrash downsides."

Exhibit 2-2 Real Estate Capital Market Balance Forecast, 2015 versus 2014

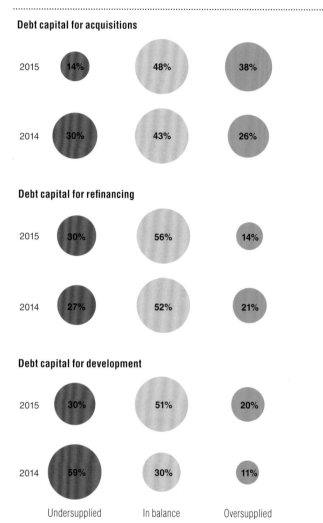

Debt capital for acquisitions

	Undersupplied	In balance	Oversupplied
2015	14%	48%	38%
2014	30%	43%	26%

Debt capital for refinancing

	Undersupplied	In balance	Oversupplied
2015	30%	56%	14%
2014	27%	52%	21%

Debt capital for development

	Undersupplied	In balance	Oversupplied
2015	30%	51%	20%
2014	59%	30%	11%

Source: *Emerging Trends in Real Estate* surveys.
Note: Based on U.S. respondents only.

Exhibit 2-3 Debt Underwriting Standards Forecast for the United States

	Less rigorous	Remain the same	More rigorous
2015	45.7%	44.7%	9.6%
2014	43.3%	39.4%	17.4%
2013	19.6%	41.5%	39.1%
2012	31.9%	35.1%	33.0%
2011	29.8%	29.2%	41.0%

Source: *Emerging Trends in Real Estate* surveys.
Note: Based on U.S. respondents only.

Exhibit 2-4 U.S. CMBS Issuance

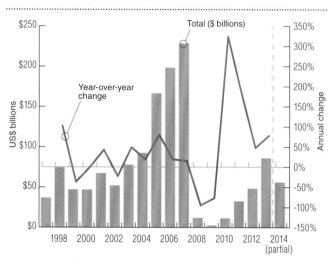

Source: *Commercial Mortgage Alert.*
*Total issuance through August 30, 2014.

Fears of a refinance crisis in 2015–2017 have subsided. That threat was widely bruited about some years ago because of the surge of issuance in 2005–2007, much of it as malodorous as week-old fish. Special servicers worked through that mess, and losses were taken right through the stack of tranches. A private equity fund manager said, "Despite the bulge in CMBS re-fis in years ahead, there doesn't seem to be a crisis brewing. The market-pricing rebound has taken a lot of the sting away. Also, not all the remaining CMBS are 'dogs'—some are, no doubt, but that's a pricing, not a volume, issue."

Quite a few interviewees worried about the concentration of CMBS new issuance in properties of lesser quality and in secondary markets early in the year. But as 2014 turned into the warmer months, more and more of this securitized debt was backed by big properties in the biggest markets. A top New York–based mortgage banker observed, "It's hard to get one bank or even a group of them to write big mortgages." It's the "lumpiness" of real estate that securitization can address, and it is more efficient to deal with an investment banking team structuring a public offering than it is to pull together a bank consortium to agree on a jointly funded loan of $500 million or more. And, yes, that means that single-asset CMBS is making a comeback.

So why the worries? A shopping center executive is concerned as he sees CMBS underwriting standards, terms and conditions, and pricing "all getting thinner." A veteran of many cycles from the valuation perspective doesn't like the return of so much "interest-only" paper. Others fret that CMBS is once again "pushing the envelope," taking deals that banks and life companies won't accept, understanding that rating agencies have pretty successfully resisted regulatory reform since 2008. As one private equity investor put it, "I really start to worry when Wall Street takes over as a leading competitor in lending."

Competition in this sector has certainly been increasing, and there are 40 or more originators supplying product at this point. It's hard to see how anyone makes money, according to one interviewee. Unfortunately, there is one way and it is tried and true: go for volume over quality, book fees, and get out fast. The advice of one institutional investment adviser is worth noting: "Watch out for assets in CMBS that are not refinanceable. Will people really want to be betting on or owning RE [real estate] in the suburbs of Iowa City?"

The quality-versus-quantity dilemma is already upon us. Throughout the industry, this will be a subject of discussion and debate in 2015 and beyond—and not just in the realm of CMBS.

Insurance Companies

"The most disciplined lenders in the business." Fifty billion dollars to $60 billion in loans, year in and year out. "Absolutely nothing has changed this year compared to last year, and nothing will change next year [either]." They have the pick of the projects, and only strong sponsors with well-leased properties in top-tier markets need apply.

Emerging Trends survey respondents see solid profitability for life company lenders going forward, and therefore are expecting a moderate increase in lending volume. But going crazy? Not these guys, say the real estate pros.

An institutional investment manager gets behind the numbers this way: "Life companies have more than enough capital and with stronger equities markets are not hobbled by allocation constraints [the denominator effect]. The NAIC's 'modified experience factor' on reserves is allowing spreads to come down, maybe too much. Spreads are now inside 100 basis points [bps] in loan quotes. This can't be sustained; 130 to 140 bps is normal."

Insurance companies are portfolio lenders, and while they care about interest rate risk they are more inclined to look at performance to maturity than at the nominal swings in prices implied by bond market volatility. Like others, insurers are forming club investment vehicles to access larger deals, so they can put out funds efficiently and compete for high-quality property loans with the public market players.

Exhibit 2-5 Availability of Capital for Real Estate, 2015 versus 2014

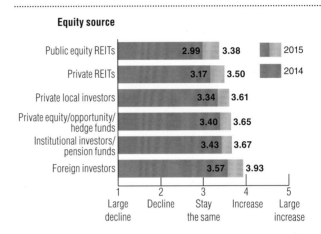

Equity source

Source	2015	2014
Public equity REITs	2.99	3.38
Private REITs	3.17	3.50
Private local investors	3.34	3.61
Private equity/opportunity/hedge funds	3.40	3.65
Institutional investors/pension funds	3.43	3.67
Foreign investors	3.57	3.93

1 Large decline — 2 Decline — 3 Stay the same — 4 Increase — 5 Large increase

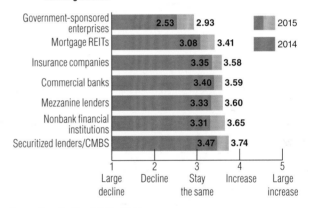

Lending source

Source	2015	2014
Government-sponsored enterprises	2.53	2.93
Mortgage REITs	3.08	3.41
Insurance companies	3.35	3.58
Commercial banks	3.40	3.59
Mezzanine lenders	3.33	3.60
Nonbank financial institutions	3.31	3.65
Securitized lenders/CMBS	3.47	3.74

1 Large decline — 2 Decline — 3 Stay the same — 4 Increase — 5 Large increase

Source: *Emerging Trends in Real Estate* surveys.
Note: Based on U.S. respondents only.

If "timing is everything," when should you pitch the life companies for a mortgage loan? A Chicago-based international real estate consultant thinks that the time to get the insurers' attention is early in the year: "Good for the first six months of each year, but then they are out of allocations." Others are not so sure, pointing to life company clients who still need to find deals in August and beyond before the year-end clock runs down. Data from the ACLI say unambiguously, "Don't lose sleep over this." In most years since 1990, it is the economic cycle—not the calendar itself—that shapes the quarter-to-quarter loan volume put out by the life companies. It's comforting, perhaps, to think that some variable like seasonality is the reason why an investment committee declines a mortgage bid. It is more likely the case that basic underwriting is the cause.

Unless insurers are tempted by "style drift" to compromise underwriting in the search for higher yields (a possibility not to be ignored), look for life companies to have a steady—but not a growing—presence in commercial property lending in 2015. We should actually be pleased to find these lenders steering away from turbulent waters.

REIT Debt

In a world so recently recovering from the seasick feeling of overleverage and sudden de-levering, could it be that REITs are not using borrowed capital enough? One very experienced REIT specialist thinks so. "REITs should be taking better advantage of today's low interest rates, levering up to 50 percent. Managers and REIT investors are paying too much attention to analysts whose background is in securities, not real estate. For real estate companies, debt ratios should reflect the percentage of fixed assets. REITs are just not comparable with other industries, no matter what Wall Street thinks."

At least one Wall Street insider concurs. "REITs are doing well. Metrics are good, and [are] supporting ratings upgrades. Public companies are rationalizing their portfolios and upgrading facilities. REITs are very active in the capital market: refinancing old preferred stock issuances and old bonds. REIT bond IPOs [initial public offerings] keep coming fast; there were 25 in the first half of 2014."

One trend to watch is the step-up in activity by nontraded REITs. Private mortgage REITs, for example, do not have the same regulatory constraints that bank and insurance lenders must contend with. With a growing appetite on the borrower side—more *Emerging Trends* survey respondents see oversupply of equity capital than oversupply of debt—an opportunity exists for private mortgage REITs to fill a vacuum in 2015.

Bespoke Lending

Structured finance, real estate style, is a field with nonbank banks, hedge funds, credit companies, and others crafting individual, customized financing as needed by borrowers who have to go outside the traditional channels for debt. Each transaction is styled according to the needs and the financial capacity of borrowers. The all-in costs can be in the mid- to high teens, which reflect the riskiness of this niche, and the position of lenders' being in the driver's seat. While not a trendsetter, bespoke lending nevertheless expands the margins of the financing universe and is an artifact of this era of capital abundance. Largely unregulated, deals here are rarely crafted with an eye to what happens when the real estate becomes a problem. That is an issue: long-term default studies have shown that even cautious

lenders will find 15 percent or more of their loans delinquent during their originally prescribed maturities.

Mezzanine debt is one arena where such customized lenders like to play. The present and likely future environment makes that arena pretty limited. One private equity investor virtually writes off this market segment for now: "Mezz debt is the most overstated opportunity at present. There is too much money flowing to achieve reasonable yields. This is a product better suited to dislocated market conditions. Mezz is living in the 75 percent to 85 percent LTV tier, but only able to earn less than 10 percent, with 1.10 DSC for deals priced at a 5 percent cap rate. That's way too much risk for that kind of pricing."

Last Word on Lending

"Every lender is in every other lender's business, making this environment as competitive as it has ever been."

Meanwhile, on the Equity Side . . .

You name it, a player on the real estate equity investment side wants it—and has the funds to plop on the table. Institutional investors are looking for product. REITs are looking for accretive deals, rationalizing their holdings in the process. Sovereign wealth funds are pouring money into the U.S. property markets, as are high-net-worth individuals from around the world. Private equity funds are pooling capital from "the 1 percent" and beyond to bid on the most notable of trophies but are also

Exhibit 2-6 Moody's/RCA Commercial Property Price Index, by Major/Nonmajor Markets

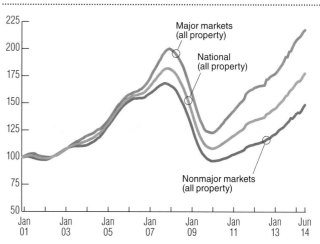

Sources: Moody's and Real Capital Analytics.

Notes: Major markets are defined here as Boston, Chicago, Los Angeles, San Francisco, New York City, and Washington, D.C. The Moody's/RCA Commercial Property Price Index is based on repeat-sales transactions that occurred at any time up through the month before the current report. Updated August 2014; data through June 2014.

scouring the country for any overlooked property opportunities. Developers are hardly deterred by higher equity requirements in the capital stack—there's just so much money around. "Everyone is in the pool." The amount of capital is "wondrous." And, for the frustrated, "There are just too many people, with too many dollars, and too few deals."

Sellers are saying, "Property is priced for perfection." Buyers are thinking, "Property is priced to disappoint." Perhaps it is time to remember the hoary anecdote of J. Pierpont Morgan and the shoeshine boy. According to Wall Street legend, when Morgan was given a "hot tip" by the lad shining his wingtips, he saw a signal that it was time to strategically exit stocks. As a savvy West Coast investor said in his *Emerging Trends* interview, some highly respected names in the real estate field think we are getting close to that time in property.

Yet the money keeps flowing. Through July 2014, acquisition volume registered by Real Capital Analytics was $215.8 billion, up 17.3 percent from the comparable period in 2013. Nearly 60 percent of survey respondents expect that the volume of equity capital will increase moderately or significantly in 2015. If true, the inflows will continue the trend of upward pressure on prices. At least one international investor in U.S. real estate expects that cap rates will fall even if interest rates rise because of capital pressures on prices. On balance, *Emerging Trends* survey respondents think that 2015 will be a year when it is better to be a seller than a buyer, but best of all this is a great time to own and hold real estate assets.

The basic "principle of anticipation" says that any investment is priced by the expected benefits of ownership into the future. The captains of real estate equity see themselves sailing toward an auspicious horizon with fair winds and following seas—at least for now. But even now many are trimming up in preparation for future squalls, with the lessons of recent hurricanes vividly in mind.

Institutional Investors

For those looking at real estate as an asset class that must perform as an element in a broader portfolio, the current term of art is *relative value*. Property investments are currently producing attractive cash flow and total returns compared with those of other alternatives, and still have the longer-run diversification advantages and inflation-hedging attributes that argue for a meaningful allocation alongside other financial vehicles. "Beta" investors face the continual challenge of putting accumulating capital to work meeting long-duration liabilities. They need adequate returns for those needs while conserving the capital entrusted to them as fiduciaries. That's a challenge indeed as the tides push all boats in the same direction and a search for

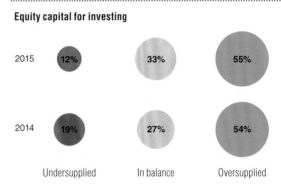

Exhibit 2-7 **Real Estate Capital Market Balance Forecast, 2015 versus 2014**

Equity capital for investing

	Undersupplied	In balance	Oversupplied
2015	12%	33%	55%
2014	19%	27%	54%

Source: *Emerging Trends in Real Estate* surveys.
Note: Based on U.S. respondents only.

yield drives managers toward "risk-on" tactics. Some are "going where they have never gone before," joining those headed for secondary markets and niche property types.

To one Midwest advisory firm, though, this doesn't seem odd. "Institutional players are climbing the ladder from core-only to higher-yielding assets, often in niche products like self-storage and senior housing, as well as to higher-risk opportunistic deals in hotels and development. This is a typical cycle, one we've seen again and again." The head of this firm says, "Raising money is not an issue. The question is policing the money. It is truly hard to find deals that pencil out now."

At least part of the challenge stems from the propensity of institutional investors to follow the very same sea lanes to the same limited number of harbors. Now that the first years of capital recovery in real estate are behind us, the elements of "core" investment—Class A properties, gateway markets, strong current income with staggered lease expirations on the rent roll—have been thoroughly netted. If you want more of those in your portfolio, you'll pay dearly. These are the "priced for perfection" properties, those where all the anticipated good news is already embedded in the price, undiscounted for potential downside risks.

"Risk-on" is not necessarily inappropriate for institutions, their conservative reputation and propensities notwithstanding. If you want to avoid risk, stick to clipping Treasury coupons. Institutions' longer time horizons and their "hold" rather than "trade" portfolio approach are actually quite consonant with accepting short-run cyclical risk and even some of the leasing risk inherent in value-add properties where repositioning can unlock potential value. It is worth remembering that in a weakening market, the most valuable attribute is a long-term lease, but in a strengthening market the most valuable attributes are vacant space to rent and expiring leases to renew.

Risk management is not the same as risk avoidance. The movement of institutional capital into noncore property investment does not necessarily betray a loss of discipline, as long as the risk/reward equation is honestly computed.

In this environment, pension funds are bound to be more hands-on, a trend already with the wind at its back. The larger the investor, the more it wants a say in decision making at all points of the investment process: at acquisition, during the operating period, and in timing disposition. As a cross-border real estate investment analyst said in his interview, we will see the "give-me-your-capital-and-trust-me approach" increasingly out of favor. With the internalization of real estate asset management at pension plans, investors will be consolidating assets with fewer external managers so that there are fewer relationships to oversee.

REITs

The real estate investment trust industry is incredibly dynamic at mid-decade, its engines humming and its bow wave creating energy in markets that all other investors must heed. REITs have broad access to capital from both private and public sources, and can choose when and where to use their entity-level power to complement a strategy of rationalizing their individual property holdings.

It is no accident that REITs have been capital magnets. That's the power of performance. As one institutional money manager said, "REITs can anticipate 3 percent to 4 percent dividend growth, and should be able to deliver 8 percent to 10 percent yield to investors as a steady flow." That's a real sweet spot right now. That manager also observed, "There's been an evolution in the way sophisticated investors see REITs. Where they were

once in the 'other investments' bucket, they first shifted to 'alternatives' and now are considered a full-fledged 'asset class.' "

A debate continues about REITs' higher correlation with common stocks lessening their diversification benefit in mixed-asset portfolios, when compared with direct investment. It is clear, however, that large-scale investors are not waiting for the outcome of that debate when they have money to put to work now. As long as the trusts' performance remains strong, they will have no trouble sourcing capital of all kinds, particularly from sources that especially value liquidity and real-time pricing.

One way that REITs have been enhancing performance has been in trimming their sails somewhat. That doesn't mean getting smaller; it means rejiggering their holdings. A veteran association executive noted, "Reinvestment is a big issue for REITs. If they can profit by selling at a 5 percent cap, what can they buy that is accretive to earnings?" It is generally pretty inefficient to tackle this question property by property if you are a public company with a market capitalization in the multiple billions. So how do you do it? By merger or corporate acquisition if you are a buyer, or by spinning off a discrete portion of your asset base if you believe the equities market will reward a wholesale reconfiguration with a premium over the net asset value (NAV) of the assets.

The trend toward such entity-level transactions should remain strong in 2015, as the REIT industry is participating in a more general tendency of public companies to rationalize and consolidate. A lot of "dry powder" is in the arsenals of American investors, and REITs—like other firms—will be maneuvering to get upwind of the opportunities.

Specialization in the REIT sector means that local markets and property types will see varying degrees of participation from the trusts. More will be discussed in the later sections of *Emerging Trends*, but this is a good place to remind ourselves that the granularity of the real estate industry always requires a look at detail. Broad trends are important, but do not necessarily apply evenly across the property universe.

Private Equity Funds

Pooling capital from high-net-worth individuals and other noninstitutional investors might at first seem to underscore the healthy diversity of the roster of commercial real estate players. There's some truth to that, but it shouldn't be overplayed. As an astute *Emerging Trends* interviewee described it, "Private wealth is increasingly thinking, acting, and being advised exactly like institutional money." Another remarked, "This is a different market from the 1980s—not doctors, lawyers, and accountants, but mostly the 1 percenters looking for a way to

Exhibit 2-8 **Equity Underwriting Standards Forecast for the United States**

	Less rigorous	Remain the same	More rigorous
2015	41.4%	47.5%	11.1%
2014	30.7%	50.8%	18.5%
2013	19.6%	50.7%	29.7%
2012	22.8%	46.7%	30.5%
2011	26.6%	40.6%	32.8%

Source: *Emerging Trends in Real Estate* surveys.
Note: Based on U.S. respondents only.

Exhibit 2-9 U.S. Buyers and Sellers: Net Capital Flows, by Source and Property Sector, 2Q 2013 – 2Q 2014

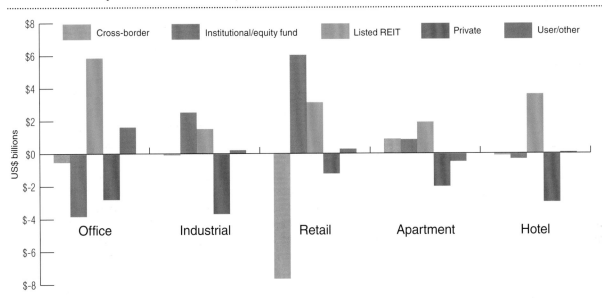

Source: Real Capital Analytics.

store value." Forbes's most recent billionaires list counted 1,645 worldwide, up 19.5 percent from 2013. The United States leads the list with 492, with many of the newcomers arriving thanks to the tech boom.

Respondents to the *Emerging Trends* survey overwhelmingly (63.1 percent) endorse the view that private equity funds (including hedge funds and opportunity funds) will see either moderate or dramatic increases in their capital in 2015. As in other equity capital sources, the tide is rising. But here we find some intriguing crosscurrents.

On one hand, capital conservation surely is a key imperative. Once you have a billion or two, you want to keep it—first and foremost; adding a couple of hundred basis points to return is lower on the priority list. On the other hand, there is a nimbleness in the private equity sector and a deal-oriented mentality that is more open to noncore properties and markets away from the gateway cities. If nothing else, the private equity sector is sensitively attuned to potential arbitrage between the institutional and noninstitutional pricing variables. For instance, a solid opportunity may be found in markets that have not yet made it to the preference lists of core and core-plus investors. One example of this was cited by an insider at one of the oldest institutional real estate funds: "The middle of the U.S. should be viewed as a favored emerging market opportunity for non-institutional investors. There is lots of 'alpha' available for those willing to go there while we stay with long-term plays in supply-constrained cities."

International Investors

It doesn't take more than basic attention to the news to sense the ramping up of international investment in U.S. real estate. From coast to coast, the Chinese, for instance, have been grabbing headlines with deals like the $1 billion acquisition by Greenland Holdings of the Metropolis project in Los Angeles from CalSTRS and its 70 percent stake in Brooklyn's 14-building Atlantic Yards development, joining Forest City Ratner. China Vanke, meanwhile, is working with Tishman Speyer in a 655-unit apartment project in the South of Market (SoMa) neighborhood in San Francisco.

Yet China is just one of many sources of inbound investment, though perhaps the most visible because of the predilection for eye-popping deals and its status as the new kid on the block. *Emerging Trends* interviewees know firsthand the breadth of the offshore equity capital rushing into the United States. A New York–based value-add owner/operator rattled off those buying pieces of his deals in the past year: "Israelis, Koreans, Egyptians, Russians, Mexicans, and others have all come to us for a piece of Manhattan."

Gateway cities are still the principal targets for offshore investors, with the list now including Houston and Seattle in addition to the big California markets, Miami, and the Boston–Washington corridor. But a boutique international investment firm says, "The heartland is now actively considered by Russian, South American, Middle Eastern, [and] Asian investors. They

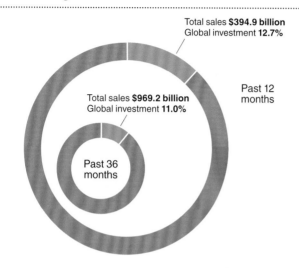

Exhibit 2-10 Global Investment in the United States as Percentage of Total Sales

Total sales **$394.9 billion**
Global investment **12.7%**

Past 12 months

Total sales **$969.2 billion**
Global investment **11.0%**

Past 36 months

Source: Real Capital Analytics, as of July 31, 2014.

like the fundamentals but are really capital [yield] driven." The integration of the world economy, on practically all imaginable levels, is one of the profound hallmarks of our time.

Despite globalization, though, there are frictions in the international investor realm that domestic capital just doesn't experience. The Foreign Investment in Real Property Tax Act (FIRPTA) has long annoyed those seeking greater fluidity in accessing offshore capital. Now Europe has joined the

game with the Alternative Investment Fund Managers Directive (AIFMD). This will potentially constrain growth in sourcing European capital by hedge funds and private equity, according to a firm with a quarter-century of experience in that business. Offerings must be vetted by European Union (E.U.) regulators and comply with disclosure requirements. New regulations are expected to reduce the number of non-E.U. investment managers raising capital in Europe. Consolidation will be coming because compliance is very expensive.

There is clearly a backlash from recent incidents of fraud, and these experiences and other abuses, and this will limit the number of "feeder funds" collecting offshore capital in the E.U. The chaos that followed the Arab Spring also brought international investors up short. A tremendous motivation exists on the part of the über-rich to keep a significant portion of their wealth anchored outside their home regions. Much more due diligence and much greater rigor have emerged in the offshore capital universe; smart money, not inexperienced money, is dominant.

Don't expect the trend for international capital to gain an increasing share of U.S. transaction volume to moderate any time soon. Asian capital, in particular, may prove the tonic that stimulates the long-deferred rise in development in the coming years.

Crowdfunding

Maybe it shouldn't be a surprise to hear such a buzz about crowdsourcing capital for real estate at a time when social media is the hot item in advertising and communications. After all, what

Exhibit 2-11 Global Investment in U.S. Real Estate, by Country

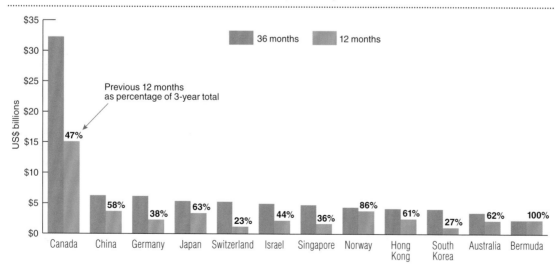

Previous 12 months as percentage of 3-year total

■ 36 months ■ 12 months

Country	%
Canada	47%
China	58%
Germany	38%
Japan	63%
Switzerland	23%
Israel	44%
Singapore	36%
Norway	86%
Hong Kong	61%
South Korea	27%
Australia	62%
Bermuda	100%

Source: Real Capital Analytics, as of July 31, 2014.

Exhibit 2-12 Global Investment in U.S. Office Sector, by Five Largest Country Sources

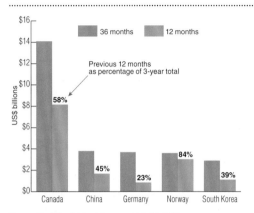

Source: Real Capital Analytics, as of July 31, 2014.

Exhibit 2-13 Global Investment in U.S. Multifamily Sector, by Five Largest Country Sources

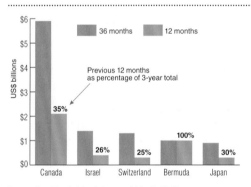

Source: Real Capital Analytics, as of July 31, 2014.

Exhibit 2-14 Global Investment in U.S. Retail Sector, by Five Largest Country Sources

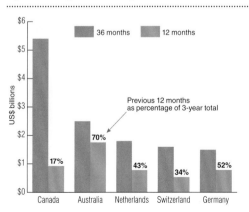

Source: Real Capital Analytics, as of July 31, 2014.

Exhibit 2-15 Global Investment in U.S. Industrial Sector, by Five Largest Country Sources

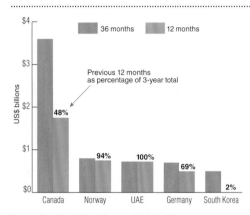

Source: Real Capital Analytics, as of July 31, 2014.

Exhibit 2-16 Global Investment in U.S. Hotel Sector, by Five Largest Country Sources

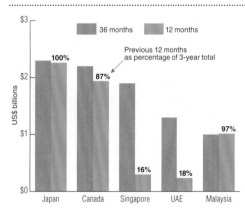

Source: Real Capital Analytics, as of July 31, 2014.

can you say when Snapchat—a site that allows the sharing of pictures that promptly disappear after viewing—is reputedly valued at $10 billion (about the same as Garmin) despite the absence of revenue? Maybe there should be less fear about asset bubbles and more about app bubbles! But we digress.

Crowdfunding is touted as a movement democratizing investment in real estate. Interviewees have seen it in action for small projects at the local level, but find it untried at scale. They expressed concern about outsourcing risk to a "crowd" ill-prepared to accept it and believe that more consumer protection and regulation lie ahead.

It does no good to just ignore the phenomenon. It is out there, and the buzz will intensify.

Nonetheless, real estate practitioners appear skeptical. A developer in the Southeast called it "a technology trend. Weird, and a potential disaster because real estate doesn't always go up. Once you have a problem, you need to know your partners." And a more traditional capital intermediary believes, "If I told my partners that I was putting them alongside crowdsourced capital, they would say, 'It's been nice doing business with you. Good luck.' "

The View from the Bridge

The captains of the real estate industry are celebrating the economy and the industry's rising tide. Chastened by the shipwrecks of the recent past, though, both equity and debt investors are disinclined to push the throttle to "all ahead full." Rather, all are seeking to pilot their way carefully, recognizing the opportunities and risks provided in the market, while respecting the respective strengths and weaknesses of the resources under their command.

Keeping in mind the adage "red sky at night, sailor's delight," investors are encouraged by the strengthening economic signs accumulating as 2014 has advanced. They take them as a sign of a trend of further fundamental improvement in markets during 2015. If the capital markets have gotten ahead of the fundamental markets in this cycle—a fair assessment—the trend toward a closer alignment may be one of the most significant developments in the coming year.

One thing is for sure: no one is inclined to ride at anchor at this point. Capital is on the move—ready, willing, and able to be put to work in real estate. Lessons learned during the Great Recession will not soon be forgotten, but it is "anchors aweigh" for real estate, which appears to be taking to heart advice from President Franklin Delano Roosevelt generations ago:

> To reach a port we must set sail—
> Sail, not tie at anchor
> Sail, not drift. [Fireside chat, April 14, 1938]

Markets to Watch

"It's no longer just about the current strength of the market or submarket. We have to be sure that the location will be viable five years from now."

Real estate investment is not immune to the economic laws of supply and demand; and as more capital flows into the asset class, two main scenarios present themselves. The first is that competition for desired assets increases, driving up prices and lowering returns. The second is that capital begins to look for alternative investments where there is less competition. *Emerging Trends in Real Estate 2015* interviewees and survey respondents offered opinions supporting the view that both scenarios are likely to influence the market in 2015.

Real estate investors continue to be willing to pay what either are or quickly will be record prices for assets in the major markets in the United States. The rationale offered by interviewees is that these markets offer a surety of return of capital that can be reproduced only in a limited number of markets across the globe. Global and domestic capital continues to be attracted to these markets. One institutional adviser referred to this as "flight capital." These investors are interested in making sure their money is placed somewhere that at an undetermined point in the future they or their heirs can be sure they can get it back. Institutional investors looking at balancing risk and return are quick to admit that "there are a lot of great opportunities for real estate investment outside the major markets, but our ability to pursue those investments is limited by the benchmarks that are used to measure our performance."

This year, interviewees and survey participants reflected a desire to take on a measured amount of new risk in search of higher yields. Two strategies mentioned repeatedly during interviews focused on moving to more opportunistic-style investments in the major markets or in markets close to a major metropolitan area (think New York City boroughs), or looking for the best assets in markets outside of the core major markets. This year's market rankings reflect the attractiveness of markets

for both of these strategies. In addition, the survey results reveal an expanded set of markets that may allow investors to find good investment opportunities outside the traditional 20 to 25 top markets. This year's interviewees continued a trend that has been expressed over the past several years. "It is important to remember that you can find good opportunities in every market, but it really helps to have the right local partner!"

To help bring out the potential strengths or weaknesses in a wider set of markets, this year's survey asked participants to rank local markets based on a set of characteristics that can often contribute to investment success, but are less influenced by macroeconomic and demographic factors that tend to favor larger, fast-growing markets. The result is a more robust view of characteristics across a wider range of markets that—when combined with 2015's emerging trends—could influence where investors choose to look for returns in the coming year.

2015 Market Rankings

"It isn't enough to pick the right market anymore. We have to pick the right market that is going to be sustainable." This sentiment, presented by a pension fund adviser, represented the thoughts of a number of interviewees. This look toward the future is clearly reflected in 2015's market rankings.

To better reflect investors' growing acceptance of a wider set of potential investment markets, a few changes have been made to improve the list of markets in this year's rankings. The total number of markets has increased to 75. The increase is the result of allowing survey respondents to select individual markets from what had historically been a more aggregate geographic area. The aggregate market groups of New York City, south Florida, and Washington, D.C., are now each represented by three markets instead of one. The Oakland/East Bay market

Exhibit 3-1 U.S. Markets to Watch: Overall Real Estate Prospects

	Investment	Development	Homebuilding
1 Houston (1, 1, 2)	4.01	3.80	4.21
2 Austin (2, 4, 1)	3.85	3.68	4.33
3 San Francisco (3, 2, 5)	3.82	3.75	3.80
4 Denver (5, 5, 4)	3.66	3.54	3.87
5 Dallas/Fort Worth (9, 8, 3)	3.56	3.43	3.98
6 Los Angeles (6, 6, 6)	3.65	3.52	3.73
7 Charlotte (7, 7, 7)	3.61	3.44	3.71
8 Seattle (4, 3, 17)	3.70	3.72	3.34
9 Boston (8, 9, 14)	3.58	3.37	3.39
10 Raleigh/Durham (16, 17, 9)	3.42	3.24	3.57
11 Atlanta (17, 15, 10)	3.40	3.25	3.54
12 Orange County (13, 14, 15)	3.50	3.27	3.36
13 Nashville (21, 12, 13)	3.32	3.35	3.40
14 New York–Manhattan (12, 10, 22)	3.44	3.36	3.26
15 San Jose (19, 19, 11)	3.33	3.21	3.50
16 Portland, OR (26, 21, 8)	3.24	3.12	3.60
17 Oakland/East Bay (11, 20, 24)	3.52	3.19	3.15
18 Chicago (14, 13, 28)	3.46	3.30	3.08
19 Miami (10, 16, 40)	3.55	3.24	2.95
20 San Diego (18, 33, 16)	3.32	3.11	3.26
21 Charleston (20, 22, 19)	3.36	2.97	3.36
22 New York–Brooklyn (15, 11, 53)	3.51	3.36	2.77
23 San Antonio (31, 30, 12)	3.12	3.00	3.43
24 Indianapolis (30, 18, 27)	3.16	3.23	3.10
25 Washington, DC–District (25, 25, 23)	3.26	3.03	3.17
26 Phoenix (23, 23, 25)	3.27	3.05	3.14
27 Philadelphia (22, 26, 34)	3.31	3.03	3.00
28 Washington, DC–Northern VA (27, 29, 31)	3.22	3.02	3.04
29 Greenville (34, 36, 20)	3.04	2.91	3.26
30 Minneapolis/St. Paul (33, 27, 29)	3.07	3.03	3.08
31 Baltimore (28, 32, 42)	3.21	2.97	2.93
32 Northern New Jersey (24, 28, 52)	3.26	3.02	2.80
33 Kansas City (46, 37, 18)	2.90	2.88	3.28
34 Columbia (32, 34, 35)	3.07	2.95	2.98
35 Tampa/St. Petersburg (36, 44, 26)	3.03	2.83	3.11
36 Salt Lake City (40, 49, 20)	2.96	2.74	3.26
37 Columbus (41, 31, 33)	2.96	2.97	3.01
38 Detroit (29, 43, 46)	3.18	2.83	2.87

	Investment	Development	Homebuilding
39 Orlando (35, 38, 43)	3.03	2.88	2.87
40 Oklahoma City (38, 24, 61)	2.99	3.04	2.69
41 St. Louis (50, 39, 36)	2.81	2.87	2.98
42 Honolulu (45, 51, 32)	2.92	2.71	3.04
43 Pittsburgh (44, 52, 30)	2.93	2.68	3.05
44 Fort Lauderdale (37, 46, 49)	3.00	2.80	2.85
45 Palm Beach (49, 45, 36)	2.82	2.81	2.98
46 Inland Empire (43, 47, 47)	2.96	2.76	2.85
47 Albuquerque (39, 41, 58)	2.98	2.84	2.75
48 New York–other boroughs (42, 48, 51)	2.96	2.76	2.80
49 New Orleans (57, 35, 50)	2.72	2.92	2.83
50 Louisville (53, 40, 54)	2.79	2.87	2.76
51 Washington, DC–MD suburbs (51, 56, 44)	2.81	2.61	2.87
52 Cleveland (48, 54, 57)	2.83	2.63	2.76
53 Madison (52, 42, 65)	2.81	2.83	2.55
54 Cincinnati (55, 53, 54)	2.75	2.65	2.76
55 Jacksonville (61, 60, 36)	2.60	2.56	2.98
56 Cape Coral/Fort Myers/Naples (54, 62, 45)	2.75	2.52	2.87
57 Des Moines (47, 50, 65)	2.85	2.71	2.55
58 Boise (59, 59, 59)	2.66	2.59	2.74
59 Birmingham (66, 55, 47)	2.52	2.61	2.85
60 Westchester/Fairfield NY/CT (58, 65, 54)	2.69	2.44	2.76
61 Omaha (60, 61, 65)	2.64	2.55	2.55
62 Tacoma (63, 66, 60)	2.56	2.43	2.72
63 Richmond (64, 63, 63)	2.54	2.51	2.62
64 Las Vegas (62, 64, 64)	2.59	2.46	2.58
65 Tucson (72, 71, 36)	2.34	2.26	2.98
66 Sacramento (73, 73, 41)	2.29	2.22	2.94
67 Spokane (67, 68, 65)	2.51	2.36	2.55
68 Portland, ME (69, 70, 62)	2.44	2.30	2.67
69 Memphis (70, 67, 70)	2.42	2.40	2.49
70 Deltona/Daytona (68, 69, 71)	2.47	2.34	2.48
71 Milwaukee (56, 58, 75)	2.75	2.60	1.84
72 Virginia Beach/Norfolk (65, 57, 74)	2.53	2.60	1.89
73 Hartford (71, 72, 72)	2.40	2.23	2.27
74 Providence (74, 74, 65)	2.16	2.00	2.55
75 Buffalo (75, 75, 73)	2.01	1.81	1.97

Source: *Emerging Trends in Real Estate 2015* survey.

Note: Numbers in parentheses are rankings for, in order, investment development, and homebuilding.

now stands alone rather than being part of San Francisco, and Tacoma, Washington, has been separated from Seattle. To better represent each of the four regions, additional markets have been added. The fast-growing South region now has seven new markets: Birmingham, Alabama; Cape Coral/Fort Myers/ Naples, Florida; Charleston, South Carolina; Columbia, South Carolina; Deltona/Daytona, Florida; Greenville, South Carolina; Louisville, Kentucky; and Richmond, Virginia. To the Midwest region the following have been added: Des Moines, Iowa; Madison, Wisconsin; and Omaha, Nebraska. The Northeast and West regions also have been expanded: Buffalo, New York; Hartford, Connecticut; and Portland, Maine, are now part of the Northeast, while Boise, Idaho, and Spokane, Washington, have been added to the West.

In an effort to get a clearer picture of how the market really feels about the markets in the survey, we asked participants to give their opinions about the 2015 outlook for each property type by market. The result is that we can get a more complete picture of the overall position of each market. The final rankings present a more complete picture of how survey participants view each market when it comes to investment, development, and the local housing market.

The results are similar to those of previous years, although we do have some repositioning of the markets. The strength of the Texas economy continues to dominate the rankings in 2015. Houston completes its ascent up the ranks and claims the number-one spot in this year's survey. Austin moves to the num-

Exhibit 3-2 **12-Month Real Estate Transaction Volume, by Market Category**

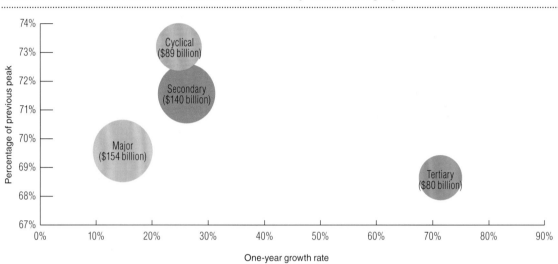

Source: Real Capital Analytics, for period ending June 30, 2014.

ber-two position, pushing perennial top market San Francisco to the number-three spot. Denver moves to the number-four spot, and the Dallas/Fort Worth market completes the Texas markets in the top 20, coming in at number five.

The remaining markets in the top 20 are composed of a combination of core major markets: Los Angeles, Boston, New York, Chicago, and markets that seem to be the first market locations that capital seeks when investors begin to look outside the core—namely, Seattle, Atlanta, and Miami. The rest of the top 20 reflect the influence of the identified emerging trends that are expected to affect the real estate market in 2015, such as Charlotte, Raleigh/Durham, Nashville, and Portland.

In the 2014 rankings, Washington, D.C., slipped out of the top ten. The survey participants do not appear to have changed their minds on the near-term outlook for D.C. In this year's survey, Washington, D.C., as represented by the District is ranked number 25. The northern Virginia suburbs of the D.C. market are ranked number 28, while the Maryland suburbs come in at number 51. New York–Manhattan experienced perhaps the most surprising move this year: the market moves to number 14. This move can be partly attributed to the fact that the New York City market is now looked at in a more granular fashion. Brooklyn comes in at number 22 and the other New York City boroughs can be found at number 48. The influence of Texas on this year's rankings has been noted, but northern California also is well represented, with San Francisco, Oakland, and San Jose all in the top 20.

Capital Flow by Market

It is one thing for survey respondents and interviewees to tell us that they are planning to be more aggressive outside the major markets; but when push comes to shove, will risk/return measures and investor expectations allow them to follow through? Using the last 12 months as a proxy for what the market may do over the next 18 months, it appears that capital will indeed continue to flow to more markets in 2015.

Exhibit 3-2 shows capital flows into markets divided into the following categories: major markets, secondary markets, cyclical markets, and tertiary markets. For clarification, the major markets are the usual suspects—New York, Boston, and Washington, D.C., among others. The secondary markets include those cities that are doing well economically, but that are typically not considered in the major category—e.g., the Texas markets, Atlanta, and Seattle. The cyclical market category is a subset of the secondary markets. It is composed of those secondary markets where capital can be deployed quickly due to the size of the market and the general level of activity. Dallas/Fort Worth and Atlanta are good examples of cyclical markets. Finally, the tertiary market category comprises all of the markets not included in the other categories.

Over the past 12 months, the major markets still continue to attract the largest dollar amount of capital, with over $154 billion invested there. This brings the major markets back to nearly 70 percent of the historical peak level of activity.

The secondary markets have seen a fairly impressive level of activity as well, totaling $140 billion. This represents nearly 72 percent of the previous peak for this group of markets. A significant portion of the investment in the secondary markets has been concentrated in the cyclical markets, with 64 percent of the investment in secondary markets going to these faster-growing locations.

Perhaps the most surprising movement—and the one that fits with the markets' desire to look for investments outside the normal locations—is the growth in capital flows to tertiary markets. The tertiary markets' share of total dollars invested is still relatively small at $80 billion, but it has seen a 72 percent growth in investment over the previous 12-month period. This rate easily outpaces any of the growth witnessed in the other categories. This pace of investment is still only 69 percent of the previous peak for these markets, so there is precedent for further investment in 2015.

A number of interviewees offered up explanations for why investment outside of the major markets may be up. The first is the belief that the economies of the housing bust markets in the South and West are now recovered to the point where it makes sense to look at investing there. This is leading to an increase in investment in markets such as the Florida markets and Phoenix. The second driver may be the desire of global capital to move outside of its typical comfort zone, which has been confined to the core major markets. An institutional adviser focused on the industrial market commented that "global investors are now seriously looking at markets such as Houston and Dallas/Fort Worth for industrial opportunities. These were markets that would have been a difficult sell to institutional investment committees in Europe and Asia just a few years ago." Finally, investors may well be going where they see the best opportunities. A retail company executive remarked, "If you don't have to worry about what your shareholders think, there are some excellent credit retail opportunities in tertiary markets. You get the same tenant credit, but the yield on the real estate is significantly higher."

Continuing Urbanization Trend

Investors continue to like markets with vibrant urban centers. The urbanization trend has been well documented in previous editions of this publication and by a host of others over the past few years. Initially, this trend clearly favored the densely populated urban cores of the major markets—New York, Boston, D.C., San Francisco, and Chicago. These markets started the race with a significant head start.

Something significant has been occurring during the recovery from the Great Recession. Cities and companies have discovered that it is possible to re-create the efficiencies and attractiveness of an urban core environment in different markets and suburban locations. This is not to say that this is an easy transformation, nor is it one that can be accomplished quickly, but it may well be worth it if you look at the relationship between urban growth and how investors are viewing 2015 market performance.

Exhibit 3-3 shows the relationship of population growth in the urban center of the markets covered in the 2015 survey and plots the growth rate against the individual market investment score. When you are examining 75 markets there are bound to be outliers, but the graphed relationship shows that the higher the urban growth rate, the more likely the market will be rated good to excellent by 2015 survey respondents.

The growth in the urban center population is clearly evident in a number of markets that are experiencing an increase in investment interest over the past year. Three notable markets that have seen significant urban growth are Austin (8.6 percent), Denver (7.6 percent), Charlotte (7.3 percent), and Seattle (6.9 percent). These markets are seeing the benefits from population growth in their urban centers and have steadily become more attractive to investors over the past three years. Survey results seem to indicate that this trend will continue in 2015.

The development of vibrant urban centers is almost a universal trend among the 75 markets included in the 2015 survey. Only five markets have seen negative growth in urban center population over the past three years. This improvement is not limited to markets that have established urban centers. Dallas/Fort Worth and Houston are two markets that historically have been identified by strong suburban growth. Interviewees made note of the development of urbanization trends that are occurring in both markets. They cited activity in the traditional downtown area and also in suburban nodes. This activity is mirroring what is normally associated with more traditional urban locations.

The next cities to benefit from increased urbanization were identified by both interviewees and survey respondents. Raleigh/Durham and Nashville, with growth rates of 5.5 percent and 4.9 percent respectively, were markets that interviewees were quick to mention as seeing good opportunity due to their increased urban feel. New Orleans, with 8.8 percent growth in its urban population, could be another city that may see improvement in investment opportunities, although survey respondents currently put the market in the fair category.

Exhibit 3-3 **Three-Year Population Growth in Urban Center, by Overall Real Estate Prospects**

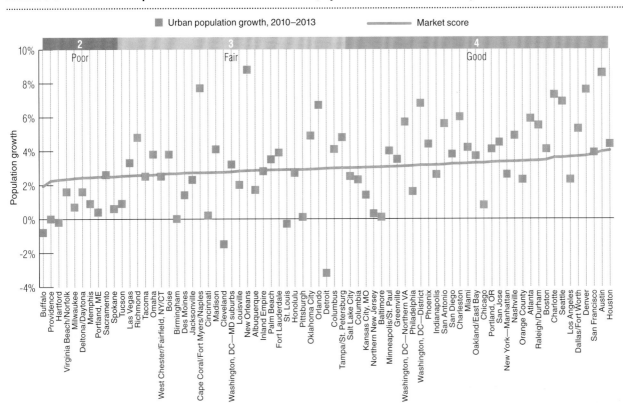

Sources: *Emerging Trends in Real Estate 2015* survey, U.S. Census Bureau.

Generational Impacts: The Potential for Change

The millennial and baby-boom generations have had a hand in a number of significant real estate changes over the decades. The baby-boom generation led the move to the suburbs during the 1960s, and the millennial generation is driving the move back to the city.

This year's interviewees were somewhat split on what choices they thought the millennial generation would make as they aged and made lifestyle decisions regarding families, employment, and future living arrangements. A real estate investment trust (REIT) executive opined: "It is likely that at least a portion of this generation will opt to move out of the city when the family starts to grow and access to extended family and schools becomes more important." Another portfolio manager offered the following opinion: "They [millennials] are so used to access to amenities and dislike the idea of commuting so much that they are just as likely to adjust their lifestyle to smaller living spaces as they are to move."

The oldest of the baby-boom generation has begun to leave the workforce, but there are still over 40 million people aged 55 to 64 who will be making work and life decisions that could have an impact on a number of areas of the real estate market. The baby-boom generation has been moving from the suburbs to the city for a number of years. One multifamily REIT executive described the options available to this generation: "A number of our tenants sold their primary residence in the suburbs and moved to an apartment in the city. They have a vacation home in a tax-favorable location, so that becomes their new primary residence but they still work and live out of the city. They enjoy being close to work, amenities, and the freedom to just get away without worrying about the house."

The result is that a number of markets will find themselves at the mercy of the decisions made by these two groups: millennials over age 30 and baby boomers ages 55 to 64. Exhibit 3-4 shows the markets with the highest exposure to these two age groups. On average, the combination of these age groups represents from 19 to 22 percent of total population of the markets in this year's survey. The exposure ranges from San Francisco

Exhibit 3-4 Millennials and Baby Boomers as Percentage of Total U.S. Population*

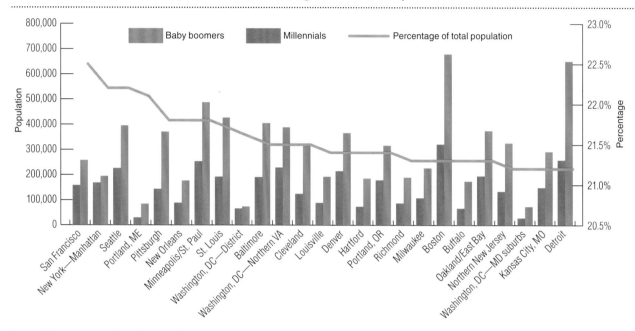

Source: U.S. Census Bureau, December 31, 2013.

*Data include only millennials who are 30 to 35 years of age and baby boomers who are 55 to 64 years of age.

with more than 397,000 people or over 21.4 percent of the total population to just across the bay in Oakland with around 525,000 representing 19.5 percent of the total population.

Markets in the Midwest could be the most affected by any potential move by the baby-boom generation. Markets such as Detroit, Minneapolis/St. Paul, and St. Louis have fairly large populations between the ages of 55 to 64. Markets with higher exposure to lifestyle decisions made by millennials between ages 30 to 35 include Detroit, Minneapolis/St. Paul, Denver, and Seattle. These groups' choices will likely have a significant impact on the type and location of the real estate they will use.

Technology and Energy Leading the Recovery

One common theme that interviewees expressed was an interest in markets with concentrations of technology- and energy-related industries. Investors are attracted to many of the characteristics that seem to accompany exposure to technology and energy industry employment.

Exhibit 3-5 illustrates the 33 markets in the *Emerging Trends in Real Estate 2015* study that have employment concentrations in technology and energy greater than the national average.

These 33 markets created more than 1.6 million jobs in the last two years, or 52 percent of the total created by all 75 markets. The resurgence in the U.S. energy industry has resulted in more growth occurring in more markets across the country. Top technology markets include San Jose; San Francisco; Washington, D.C.; Raleigh/Durham; and Seattle. Energy industry exposure is more evident in Houston, Oklahoma City, and Pittsburgh. With each geographic region represented, investors have a wide choice of markets that may offer opportunities in 2015. The projections are that energy production will continue to expand in the United States as more locations expand fracking operations. This continued expansion will drive future economic growth. Interviewees and survey respondents are confident that these industries will continue to spur growth in a number of local economies.

Jobs Go Where It Costs Less

One noted trait of the early economic recovery has been a "disconnect" between the improvement in corporate profits and a lack of higher rates of employment growth. Over the past year, the trend has reversed and employment growth has rebounded to exceed 200,000 jobs a month.

One Texas-based investor offered his opinion on the current state of job growth in the United States: "Part of the reason Texas has

Exhibit 3-5 **Technology and Energy Employment Concentration, by Market: Q2 2012 to Q2 2014**

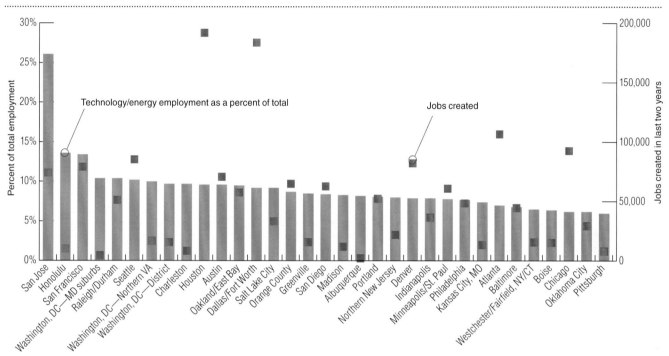

Sources: U.S. Bureau of Labor Statistics.

taken the lead in job creation is the current business-friendly environment." This business-friendly environment has resulted in four Texas markets in our survey creating 493,733 jobs over the last two years. *Business-friendly* takes into account a number of factors, but one of the most important is labor costs. A Midwest-based economist explained how the resurgence in U.S. manufacturing is benefiting the southeastern region of the country "Manufacturing is coming back to the U.S. due to rising labor costs overseas, increased problems with product quality, shipping costs and delays, and the decline in domestic energy costs. The jobs, however, are not coming back to the upper Midwest, but are going to lower-cost markets in the Southeast."

The attractiveness of lower-cost markets can be seen in the breakdown of where new jobs have been created based on market business costs. Exhibit 3-6 shows that over the past two years, more than 1.42 million jobs have been created in markets where the cost of doing business is 95 percent or lower than the national average. Markets with business costs ranging from 95 percent to 105 percent of the national average saw the creation of 1.1 million jobs.

The outlook for job growth and, by association, stronger real estate performance is best for those markets that are considered

Exhibit 3-6 **Two-Year Job Growth, by Market Cost of Doing Business**

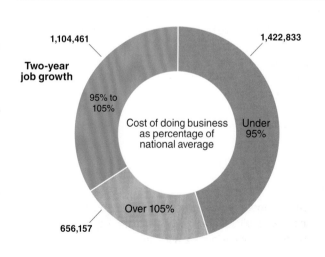

Sources: U.S. Bureau of Labor Statistics; Moody's Analytics, as of June 30, 2014.

attractive based on the metrics discussed earlier in this chapter and that have a lower-than-average cost of doing business.

The Top 20 Markets

Houston (1). Houston moves to the top spot in the 2015 survey. As one of the largest "secondary" markets, Houston offers a significant amount of investment opportunities. Investors believe that the energy industry will continue to drive market growth and that will support real estate activity in 2015.

In total, Houston was ranked number one in both investment and development expectations for next year; housing market expectations are ranked number two. The expectations for Houston real estate are high for all property sectors. Houston is ranked number one in the industrial and retail sectors; the office and multifamily sectors are ranked number two; and the hotel sector is ranked number four.

All areas of the real estate industry are interested in investment opportunities in Houston, with institutional investors particularly attracted to the city. Local market participants view the real estate market conditions as excellent in Houston for 2015, with a nearly perfect score of 4.7 out of 5.0. As expected, the local economy, real estate capital availability, and investor demand are viewed as being particularly strong for 2015.

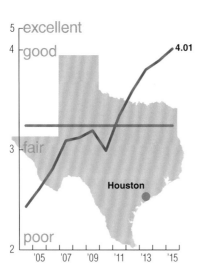

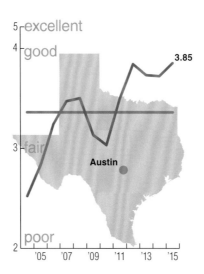

Austin (2). Austin has been a favorite of survey respondents for a number of years. Survey respondents and interviewees like the industrial base, the appeal to the millennial generation, and the lower cost of doing business in Austin.

Austin was the top choice for both the office sector and the single-family housing sector and the number-two-ranked market for retail. Austin is not a distribution hub, and this is reflected in the number-five ranking for investment in industrial. Supply concerns are also likely behind the number-six ranking for hotels and the number-12 position in the multifamily sector.

Austin also benefits from a strong level of market participation by local owner/developers. Observations from local market participants are positive for all aspects of the real estate market. Local respondents express confidence in the strength of the local economy and the level of investor demand. The availability of capital and an active local development community should guarantee a steady flow of investment opportunities in 2015.

San Francisco (3). The San Francisco market is once again at the top of the rankings, but at number three is down

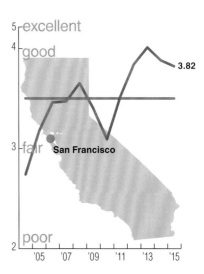

a couple of spots from last year. The consensus view expressed by interviewees and survey respondents is that the decline is likely due more to growth in the other cities than any identifiable flaw in the San Francisco market.

The strong local economy and improved domestic and international travel have made San Francisco the number-one choice for hotel investment in 2015. The other property sectors are viewed almost as favorably, with survey respondents ranking the office market number three and the retail market number four. The industrial sector is ranked number 12 in the survey. Housing also is expected to be attractive in 2015, with the multifamily sector ranked number three and the single-family sector ranked number five.

San Francisco continues to benefit from institutional investor interest in the market along with a strong private property owner/developer segment. Local market participants see the strength of the local economy driving continued strong investor demand. The availability of capital should keep deal activity high in 2015.

Denver (4). Denver joins Austin and San Francisco as markets popular with the millennial generation that appear in the

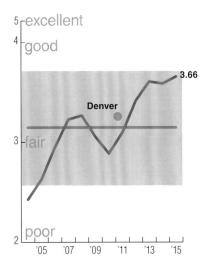

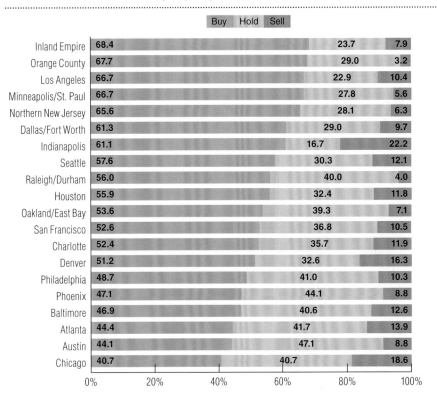

Exhibit 3-7 **U.S. Industrial Property Buy/Hold/Sell Recommendations**

	Buy	Hold	Sell
Inland Empire	68.4	23.7	7.9
Orange County	67.7	29.0	3.2
Los Angeles	66.7	22.9	10.4
Minneapolis/St. Paul	66.7	27.8	5.6
Northern New Jersey	65.6	28.1	6.3
Dallas/Fort Worth	61.3	29.0	9.7
Indianapolis	61.1	16.7	22.2
Seattle	57.6	30.3	12.1
Raleigh/Durham	56.0	40.0	4.0
Houston	55.9	32.4	11.8
Oakland/East Bay	53.6	39.3	7.1
San Francisco	52.6	36.8	10.5
Charlotte	52.4	35.7	11.9
Denver	51.2	32.6	16.3
Philadelphia	48.7	41.0	10.3
Phoenix	47.1	44.1	8.8
Baltimore	46.9	40.6	12.6
Atlanta	44.4	41.7	13.9
Austin	44.1	47.1	8.8
Chicago	40.7	40.7	18.6

0%   20%   40%   60%   80%   100%

Source: *Emerging Trends in Real Estate 2015* survey.

Note: Cities listed are the top 20 rated for investment in the industrial sector; in this exhibit, cities are ordered according to the number of "buy" recommendations.

top five of this year's survey. Denver's industry exposure to the technology and energy industries has also attracted investor interest.

Denver is the first market in the top five that does not have a property sector that respondents consider the best for 2015. The results of the survey put Denver retail at number five and office at number six. The hotel sector is number seven in this year's survey. The industrial sector has seen significant improvement in recent quarters but is still ranked number 13.

Interviewees and survey respondents have expressed some concern that the Denver market may be due for a cooling-off period in the multifamily sector. The multifamily ranking is the lowest in the market at 18. With a number-four ranking, the single-family housing sector is still expected to be strong in 2015.

Denver attracts a significant amount of interest from both public and private investors including institutional advisers, private property owners, and developers. Local market participants tout Denver's strong economy and local development community as the keys to continue to keep real estate activity up in 2015.

Dallas/Fort Worth (5). Dallas/Fort Worth rounds out the triumvirate of Texas markets in this year's top five. Interviewees raise the possibility that despite being ranked lower than Houston, the economic diversity could make the current growth rate more sustainable in Dallas/Fort Worth. The market continues to be attractive to real estate investors because of its strong job growth, which benefits from the low cost of living and doing business.

Single-family housing is the highest-ranked property sector in Dallas/Fort Worth and helped support the high overall rank. In addition, Dallas/Fort Worth has the highest-ranked industrial sector (number four) among the top five markets from this year's survey. The office sector also is expected to be strong in 2015 and is ranked number five, with hotels

coming in at number 11. Not all sectors are expected to outperform in 2015, as supply concerns seem to be driving down the ranking of the multifamily sector (number 17) and the retail sector at number 34.

Institutional investors continue to be active in Dallas/Fort Worth, but the market also benefits from being attractive to the public market as well as to both local and institutional commercial and home developers. The comparative strength of the local Dallas/Fort Worth market seems like it can be attributed to the strength of the local economy that is supported by an active and viable local development community. Investor demand remains high and there are no concerns about the availability of capital for 2015.

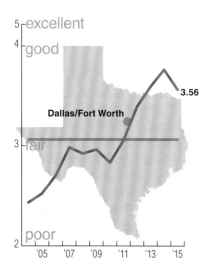

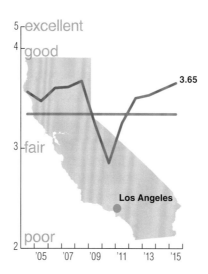

Los Angeles (6). Los Angeles is the second West Coast city in the top ten. Because it is a major market, investors are comfortable with the liquidity offered by Los Angeles. A diverse economy and the city's role as the main port of entry into the United States for goods from Asia help investors put aside concerns associated with the political climate in California.

Coming in at number two, the hotel property type is the highest-ranked sector in Los Angeles. The single-family housing market also is viewed as attractive and is ranked number six. The comparatively high cost of housing supports the multifamily market in Los Angeles, and survey respondents ranked the sector number nine. The strong industrial market is reflected in the number-ten ranking that survey respondents awarded Los Angeles for 2015. The office sector, at number 14, and retail, at number 17, round out the property sector rankings for Los Angeles.

As a major market, Los Angeles attracts interest from all segments of the real estate industry. Local market participants see investor demand and capital availability as the leading drivers of the local real estate market. Development and

redevelopment opportunities also are expected to be good in 2015.

Charlotte (7). Charlotte becomes the highest non-Texas market from the

South region in this year's survey. The Charlotte economy has rebounded from consolidation in the banking industry and is benefiting from a surge in new startup companies that have been created to service the financial services industry. Charlotte is also an attractive destination for the millennial generation and offers an appealing cost of doing business.

While Charlotte is not typically considered a distribution hub, survey respondents ranked opportunities in the industrial sector at number six in this year's survey. The industrial market is clearly benefiting from growth in the local economy. The single-family housing market has been comparatively affordable in Charlotte, but the housing market has also witnessed more residents moving back to areas near the urban center. Survey respondents put the single-family housing

Exhibit 3-8 U.S. Multifamily Property Buy/Hold/Sell Recommendations

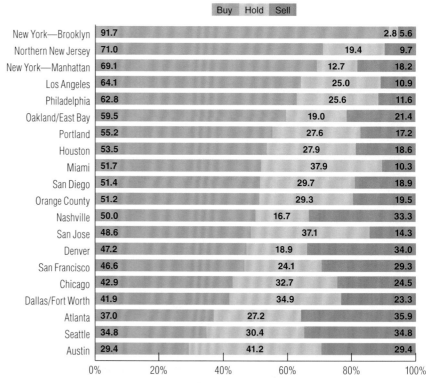

Source: *Emerging Trends in Real Estate 2015* survey.

Note: Cities listed are the top 20 rated for investment in the multifamily sector; in this exhibit, cities are ordered according to the number of "buy" recommendations.

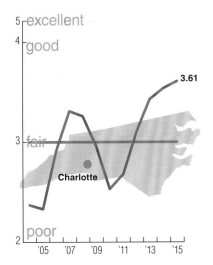

market at number seven for 2015. The hotel sector is the second-highest-ranked sector in Charlotte at number eight. This sector is benefiting from an increase in business and leisure travel. Some concern exists that multifamily supply may be a problem in 2015 and the survey reflects this, ranking the sector at number 28. The office and retail sectors in Charlotte are both respectable, with ranks of number 12 and number ten respectively.

Institutional investors continue to be active in Charlotte, but the market also benefits from being attractive to the public market as well as to both local and institutional commercial and home developers. Local market participants see the strength of the local economy and good credit availability as the strongest aspects of the local real estate market. Investor demand also is expected to be good in 2015, which could keep the local development community busy looking for opportunities.

Seattle (8). Seattle is the third West Coast market in the survey's top ten this year. Multiple interviewees commented on the amazing amount of activity the technology industry is driving in downtown Seattle. The city also remains attractive to the millennial generation and continues to attract a highly skilled labor force.

Exhibit 3-9 U.S. Office Property Buy/Hold/Sell Recommendations

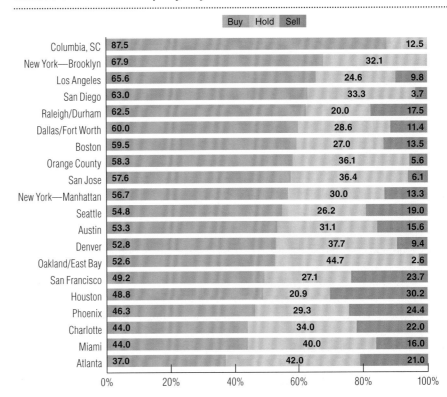

Legend: Buy | Hold | Sell

City	Buy	Hold	Sell
Columbia, SC	87.5		12.5
New York—Brooklyn	67.9	32.1	
Los Angeles	65.6	24.6	9.8
San Diego	63.0	33.3	3.7
Raleigh/Durham	62.5	20.0	17.5
Dallas/Fort Worth	60.0	28.6	11.4
Boston	59.5	27.0	13.5
Orange County	58.3	36.1	5.6
San Jose	57.6	36.4	6.1
New York—Manhattan	56.7	30.0	13.3
Seattle	54.8	26.2	19.0
Austin	53.3	31.1	15.6
Denver	52.8	37.7	9.4
Oakland/East Bay	52.6	44.7	2.6
San Francisco	49.2	27.1	23.7
Houston	48.8	20.9	30.2
Phoenix	46.3	29.3	24.4
Charlotte	44.0	34.0	22.0
Miami	44.0	40.0	16.0
Atlanta	37.0	42.0	21.0

Source: *Emerging Trends in Real Estate 2015* survey.

Note: Cities listed are the top 20 rated for investment in the office sector; in this exhibit, cities are ordered according to the number of "buy" recommendations.

Survey respondents are very positive in their outlook for the commercial real estate sector in Seattle. This optimism is reflected in the individual survey rankings by property type, with industrial coming in at number two, hotel at number three, and office at number four. If any hesitation about investments in Seattle exists, it seems focused on the housing market. The multifamily sector is ranked at number ten, while the single-family housing market is number 17.

Seattle is one of the top capital destinations outside the core major markets, and as such is very attractive to institutional and local investors alike. Local market participants are very positive on the real estate market. They feel that the strength of the local economy will continue to support good investor demand that will

be facilitated by the availability of capital. The local development community is viewed as being a positive for the market, and the market has benefited from strong public/private cooperation.

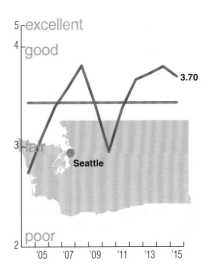

Edmonton
2

Saskatoon
8

Calgary
1

Winnipeg
7

Vancouver
4

Seattle
8

Tacoma
62

Spokane
67

Portland, OR
16

Boise
58

Minneapolis/
St. Paul
30

Sacramento
66

Salt Lake City
36

Omaha
61

Des Moines
57

San Francisco
3

Oakland—
East Bay
17

San Jose
15

Denver
4

Kansas City
33

Las Vegas
64

Albuquerque
47

Oklahoma City
40

Los Angeles
6

Inland Empire
46

Phoenix
26

Orange County
12

San Diego
20

Tucson
65

Dallas/Fort Worth
5

Honolulu/Hawaii
42

Austin
2

Houston
1

San Antonio
23

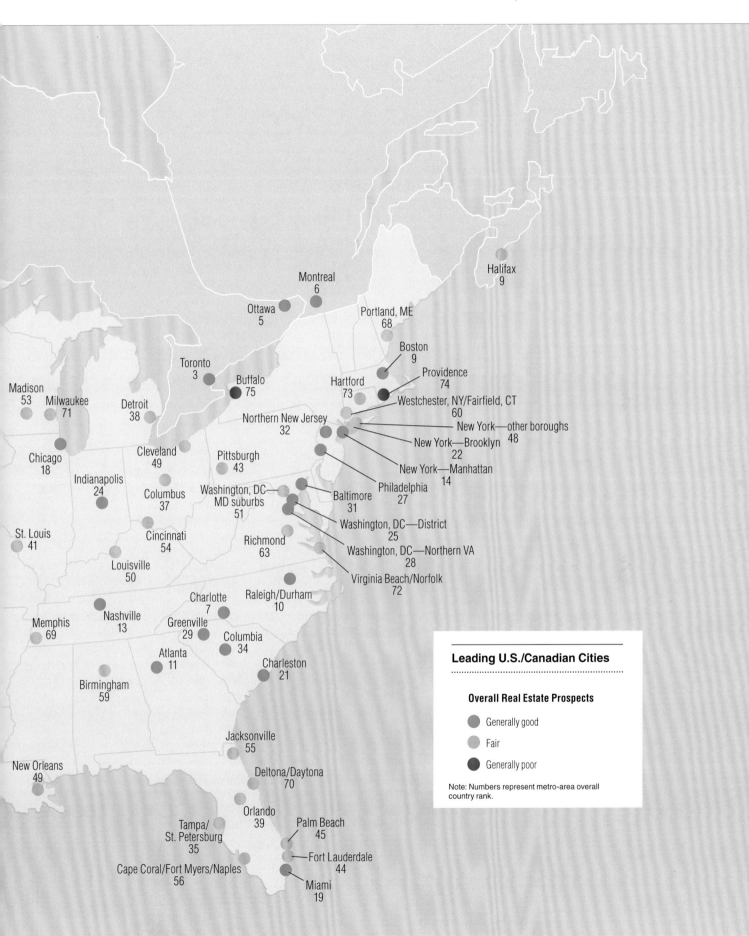

Madison 53
Milwaukee 71
Detroit 38
Toronto 3
Buffalo 75
Montreal 6
Ottawa 5
Portland, ME 68
Halifax 9
Boston 9
Hartford 73
Providence 74
Westchester, NY/Fairfield, CT 60
New York—other boroughs 48
New York—Brooklyn 22
New York—Manhattan 14
Northern New Jersey 32
Chicago 18
Cleveland 49
Pittsburgh 43
Indianapolis 24
Columbus 37
Washington, DC MD suburbs 51
Baltimore 31
Philadelphia 27
Washington, DC—District 25
Washington, DC—Northern VA 28
St. Louis 41
Cincinnati 54
Richmond 63
Louisville 50
Virginia Beach/Norfolk 72
Memphis 69
Nashville 13
Charlotte 7
Raleigh/Durham 10
Greenville 29
Columbia 34
Atlanta 11
Birmingham 59
Charleston 21
Jacksonville 55
New Orleans 49
Deltona/Daytona 70
Orlando 39
Tampa/St. Petersburg 35
Palm Beach 45
Fort Lauderdale 44
Cape Coral/Fort Myers/Naples 56
Miami 19

Leading U.S./Canadian Cities

Overall Real Estate Prospects

Generally good

Fair

Generally poor

Note: Numbers represent metro-area overall country rank.

Table 3-1 Economy

Market	2015 Population Total (millions)	2014–2015 % change	5-year annual net migration (000s)	Millennials (Age 20–35) % of total population	5-year growth	2015 GMP per capita ratio*	GMP per capita 5-year projected growth	Cost of doing business**	Per capita disposable income ratio***	5-year disposable income growth	Employment Total 2014–2015 %change	2015 as % of previous peak	2017 as % of previous peak	Bus & professional services	Education & health services	Energy	Goods producing	Office using
United States	321.34	0.8%	—	21.2%	10.6%	1.00	7.3%	100%	1.00	9.6%	2.7%	101.4%	107.6%	1.0	1.0	1.0	1.0	1.0
Albuquerque	0.90	0.2%	0.19	21.0%	-4.1%	0.78	4.8%	88.0%	0.74	4.5%	0.1%	92.6%	94.2%	0.9	1.0	0.4	0.8	0.9
Atlanta	5.69	1.6%	16.40	20.5%	16.6%	0.93	12.5%	90.0%	0.86	8.2%	2.7%	101.4%	109.2%	1.2	0.8	1.1	0.9	1.1
Austin	2.00	2.5%	8.09	24.6%	18.1%	0.99	5.9%	101.0%	0.90	9.3%	4.1%	116.1%	128.9%	1.0	0.7	0.5	1.0	1.0
Baltimore	2.82	0.7%	3.20	21.3%	8.7%	1.12	8.0%	104.0%	1.09	6.5%	2.6%	104.2%	109.8%	1.0	1.2	0.7	0.8	0.9
Birmingham	1.15	0.6%	1.46	19.8%	9.7%	0.84	12.9%	94.0%	0.86	11.4%	1.8%	95.5%	102.0%	0.8	0.9	0.7	1.1	0.9
Boise	0.67	1.6%	1.59	19.7%	8.2%	0.75	6.3%	79.0%	0.75	5.7%	3.1%	101.8%	108.4%	0.8	1.0	0.3	1.3	0.8
Boston	4.79	0.9%	5.35	21.7%	10.9%	1.36	7.6%	120.0%	1.21	8.3%	2.1%	103.2%	107.8%	1.1	1.3	0.8	0.9	1.1
Buffalo	1.13	-0.2%	-0.65	20.3%	2.8%	1.15	11.5%	89.0%	0.84	8.7%	2.3%	100.3%	103.9%	0.8	1.1	1.7	1.1	0.8
Cape Coral/Fort Myers/ Naples	1.06	2.6%	7.79	15.4%	17.3%	0.62	10.0%	95.0%	1.03	10.8%	3.8%	97.0%	106.8%	0.8	0.8	0.1	0.9	0.8
Charleston	0.73	1.3%	1.75	23.0%	12.8%	0.77	3.6%	95.0%	0.83	6.2%	2.6%	104.6%	110.6%	0.9	0.8	0.8	1.1	0.8
Charlotte	1.95	2.1%	8.88	20.5%	23.4%	0.98	3.8%	86.0%	0.87	5.1%	2.9%	104.1%	112.2%	1.1	0.6	1.4	1.1	1.1
Chicago	9.62	0.4%	-3.84	21.1%	7.2%	1.04	9.4%	99.0%	0.96	8.1%	1.8%	98.1%	102.1%	1.1	1.0	1.7	1.1	1.0
Cincinnati	2.18	0.6%	1.24	19.7%	8.6%	0.90	6.2%	95.0%	0.89	7.7%	2.7%	100.1%	105.4%	1.0	1.0	1.7	1.3	0.9
Cleveland	2.05	-0.3%	-2.15	18.2%	3.2%	1.01	7.8%	97.0%	0.94	8.9%	2.7%	96.8%	101.6%	0.9	1.2	2.1	1.4	0.8
Columbia	0.82	1.5%	2.85	22.2%	14.0%	0.81	2.2%	93.0%	0.77	6.5%	2.8%	100.4%	106.7%	0.8	0.8	1.8	1.0	0.9
Columbus	1.94	0.7%	1.02	22.2%	9.6%	1.00	2.6%	95.0%	0.88	7.4%	2.4%	105.6%	111.0%	1.0	0.9	1.1	0.9	1.0
Dallas/Fort Worth	7.08	2.0%	22.10	21.2%	16.0%	1.07	14.2%	94.0%	0.96	9.7%	3.8%	108.4%	118.9%	1.0	0.8	1.0	1.2	1.0
Deltona/Daytona	0.52	2.0%	3.43	16.8%	13.5%	0.56	9.6%	86.0%	0.72	10.9%	3.7%	94.1%	102.5%	0.7	1.3	0.4	0.9	0.7
Denver	2.81	1.7%	8.31	21.8%	15.9%	1.08	7.3%	94.0%	1.04	9.4%	3.2%	107.2%	115.5%	1.1	0.8	0.5	1.0	1.1
Des Moines	0.61	0.5%	-0.09	20.9%	6.8%	1.17	14.6%	83.0%	0.99	8.3%	3.1%	105.7%	112.0%	0.8	0.9	1.1	0.9	1.2
Detroit	4.28	-0.1%	-2.71	18.6%	4.8%	0.90	11.3%	95.8%	0.90	8.8%	2.8%	91.7%	96.5%	1.2	1.0	1.2	1.3	1.0
Fort Lauderdale	1.90	1.5%	6.87	19.5%	14.2%	0.79	3.4%	96.0%	0.91	10.5%	3.1%	98.8%	106.1%	1.1	0.8	0.3	0.7	1.1
Greenville	0.68	1.1%	1.67	20.5%	12.0%	0.79	8.7%	90.0%	0.78	7.1%	2.8%	102.2%	108.5%	1.2	0.7	4.9	1.4	1.0
Hartford	1.22	0.0%	-0.20	19.5%	6.9%	1.50	11.1%	102.0%	1.09	10.8%	2.2%	98.4%	102.8%	0.7	1.1	0.7	1.2	1.0
Honolulu	1.00	0.9%	0.75	23.7%	8.1%	1.05	4.8%	116.0%	1.03	5.8%	1.7%	100.8%	103.9%	0.9	0.9	0.2	0.7	0.8
Houston	6.61	1.7%	13.71	21.8%	13.7%	1.29	19.8%	99.0%	1.10	10.1%	3.8%	112.1%	122.6%	0.9	0.8	2.2	1.7	0.8
Indianapolis	1.87	1.2%	2.36	20.5%	13.2%	1.04	5.0%	87.0%	0.89	8.8%	2.2%	104.1%	109.5%	1.0	0.9	2.3	1.2	0.9
Inland Empire	4.49	1.2%	4.78	21.9%	11.1%	0.62	4.8%	92.0%	0.65	9.9%	2.6%	98.6%	103.8%	0.7	1.0	1.1	1.1	0.6
Jacksonville	1.43	1.3%	3.96	20.8%	11.7%	0.80	6.6%	91.0%	0.89	11.1%	2.9%	100.0%	107.0%	1.0	0.9	0.3	0.8	1.1
Kansas City, MO	2.12	0.8%	1.78	20.0%	9.5%	0.92	8.5%	89.0%	0.94	8.2%	2.7%	100.2%	105.7%	1.0	0.9	1.2	1.0	1.0
Las Vegas	2.12	2.2%	10.12	21.4%	20.3%	0.80	2.7%	85.0%	0.78	9.4%	3.1%	95.4%	103.4%	0.8	0.6	0.3	0.7	0.8
Los Angeles	10.16	0.6%	2.12	23.5%	9.3%	1.14	8.7%	103.0%	0.90	10.4%	2.6%	99.6%	105.3%	0.9	1.2	0.9	1.0	1.0
Louisville	1.33	0.6%	1.39	19.6%	10.1%	0.87	7.5%	85.0%	0.88	8.2%	2.7%	102.3%	107.6%	0.8	0.9	1.4	1.4	0.8
Madison	0.60	1.0%	0.76	24.3%	6.4%	1.19	9.9%	94.0%	1.05	11.0%	2.4%	104.1%	109.4%	0.7	0.7	1.8	1.1	0.9
Memphis	1.36	0.7%	1.04	20.8%	10.9%	0.85	5.3%	85.0%	0.87	6.9%	2.6%	96.4%	101.6%	0.9	0.9	1.3	1.0	0.8
Miami	2.66	0.9%	6.64	21.1%	12.1%	0.79	1.9%	107.0%	0.85	10.2%	2.9%	103.3%	110.1%	0.9	1.0	0.5	0.6	0.9
Milwaukee	1.57	0.2%	-0.61	20.2%	2.9%	0.98	8.5%	99.0%	0.98	11.3%	2.1%	97.5%	101.9%	0.9	1.2	1.3	1.5	0.9

Sources: Moody's Analytics, U.S. Census Bureau, Bureau of Economic Analysis, Bureau of Labor Statistics.

*Metro GMP per capita/National GMP per capita.

**Cost of doing business - national average = 100%.

***Market per capita disposable income/national per capita disposable income.

****Location quotient measures employment concentration by market - (metro industry employment as a % of metro total)/(national indsustry employment as a % of national total).

Table 3-1 Economy

Market	2015 Population Total (millions)	2014–2015 % change	5-year annual net migration (000s)	Millennials (Age 20–35) % of total population	5-year growth	2015 GMP per capita ratio*	GMP per capita 5-year projected growth	Cost of doing business**	Per capita disposable income ratio***	5-year disposable income growth	Employment Total 2014–2015 % change	2015 as % of previous peak	2017 as % of previous peak	Bus & professional services	Education & health services	Energy	Goods producing	Office using
United States	321.34	0.8%	—	21.2%	10.6%	1.00	7.3%	100%	1.00	9.6%	2.7%	101.4%	107.6%	1.0	1.0	1.0	1.0	1.0
Minneapolis/St. Paul	3.47	0.9%	2.57	20.9%	7.4%	1.08	7.7%	99.0%	1.00	0.6%	2.0%	101.2%	105.8%	0.9	1.1	1.2	1.2	1.0
Nashville	1.71	0.8%	1.16	21.9%	11.4%	0.97	3.3%	90.0%	1.00	7.2%	3.1%	109.7%	116.0%	1.0	1.0	0.8	1.2	1.0
New Orleans	1.23	0.4%	0.07	21.7%	4.8%	0.98	7.6%	86.0%	0.94	11.0%	3.0%	91.2%	96.8%	0.8	1.0	1.8	1.1	0.8
New York—Brooklyn	2.64	0.7%	-2.37	26.0%	11.0%	1.27	7.3%	140.0%	0.91	19.6%	2.3%	110.5%	116.9%	0.5	2.3	0.2	0.3	0.8
New York—other boroughs	7.11	0.3%	-4.03	21.0%	6.3%	1.27	7.3%	140.0%	1.49	15.8%	2.2%	105.2%	110.1%	0.7	1.5	0.9	0.7	0.8
New York—Manhattan	1.65	0.3%	-1.17	30.9%	6.2%	1.27	7.3%	160.0%	2.65	19.2%	1.8%	104.0%	108.7%	1.3	0.8	0.0	0.1	1.5
Northern New Jersey	2.17	0.1%	-1.33	18.5%	7.5%	1.20	5.0%	102.0%	1.05	20.5%	2.7%	95.9%	100.9%	1.1	1.0	2.2	0.8	1.0
Oakland/East Bay	2.71	0.7%	1.98	21.1%	10.6%	1.00	4.1%	104.0%	1.21	11.0%	2.9%	100.4%	107.1%	1.0	1.1	1.2	1.1	0.9
Oklahoma City	1.36	1.3%	2.50	22.5%	11.3%	0.90	7.1%	83.0%	0.92	7.9%	2.5%	107.7%	113.3%	0.8	0.9	0.4	1.2	0.8
Omaha	0.92	1.4%	1.91	21.1%	12.3%	0.98	1.6%	89.0%	0.97	3.9%	3.0%	102.2%	109.0%	0.9	1.0	1.1	1.0	1.0
Orange County	3.18	0.9%	2.22	21.6%	9.9%	1.31	6.9%	102.0%	1.05	10.2%	2.9%	97.6%	103.6%	1.1	0.8	1.1	1.4	1.1
Orlando	2.39	2.4%	13.68	22.2%	18.9%	0.87	0.7%	94.0%	0.76	10.2%	3.1%	102.9%	111.5%	1.0	0.8	0.3	0.7	1.0
Palm Beach	1.43	2.3%	10.00	17.0%	17.6%	0.76	2.5%	96.0%	1.17	10.7%	3.5%	98.6%	107.6%	1.1	1.0	0.2	0.7	1.0
Philadelphia	6.07	0.3%	-0.26	20.6%	5.8%	1.01	6.8%	105.0%	1.06	8.5%	2.4%	99.0%	104.0%	1.0	1.3	1.5	0.9	1.0
Phoenix	4.60	2.3%	20.37	20.8%	17.7%	0.81	8.2%	93.0%	0.79	9.0%	3.1%	95.8%	103.5%	1.0	1.0	0.4	1.0	1.1
Pittsburgh	2.36	0.1%	1.84	18.9%	4.5%	1.03	5.1%	94.0%	1.00	9.7%	2.5%	101.9%	106.9%	0.9	1.3	1.0	1.1	0.9
Portland, ME	0.52	0.4%	2.70	17.4%	0.4%	0.88	7.1%	106.0%	0.95	5.3%	2.0%	99.8%	104.4%	0.8	1.2	1.0	1.1	0.8
Portland, OR	2.36	0.9%	0.44	21.0%	9.5%	1.25	9.3%	94.0%	0.92	12.5%	3.1%	103.4%	110.3%	0.9	1.0	0.7	1.4	0.9
Providence	1.61	0.2%	0.47	20.1%	7.3%	0.86	5.4%	100.0%	0.94	4.9%	2.0%	97.1%	100.8%	0.7	1.4	1.2	1.2	0.7
Raleigh/Durham	2.32	1.7%	7.97	20.7%	20.5%	0.97	8.1%	85.1%	0.87	6.5%	3.1%	104.7%	113.3%	1.1	1.0	1.5	1.0	1.0
Richmond	1.32	0.8%	1.61	20.7%	11.2%	0.99	7.5%	90.0%	0.91	7.8%	2.1%	101.7%	106.4%	1.0	0.9	1.2	0.9	1.0
Sacramento	2.27	1.0%	2.65	21.5%	9.8%	1.01	6.5%	96.0%	0.91	11.1%	3.2%	97.6%	104.4%	0.8	1.0	0.3	0.8	0.8
Salt Lake City	1.21	1.3%	1.04	23.5%	13.8%	1.15	8.8%	84.0%	0.88	7.9%	3.7%	107.1%	115.4%	1.0	0.7	1.1	1.2	1.0
San Antonio	2.38	1.9%	6.67	21.8%	13.1%	0.78	8.8%	84.0%	0.83	9.5%	3.6%	110.2%	120.1%	0.8	1.0	0.4	0.9	0.9
San Diego	3.30	1.2%	2.96	24.6%	10.0%	1.11	6.2%	111.0%	1.01	9.9%	2.6%	102.6%	108.2%	1.1	0.9	0.9	1.1	0.9
San Francisco	1.88	0.9%	2.37	23.0%	11.4%	1.71	6.8%	118.0%	1.57	10.6%	3.0%	109.2%	116.2%	1.4	0.9	1.0	0.6	1.4
San Jose	1.94	0.6%	-0.20	21.6%	10.6%	1.52	7.5%	116.0%	1.45	11.0%	3.0%	108.0%	114.8%	1.2	1.0	0.3	1.7	1.2
Seattle	2.88	1.3%	4.05	22.6%	12.0%	1.48	7.9%	101.0%	1.22	4.6%	2.6%	104.3%	110.2%	0.9	0.8	0.3	1.4	1.0
Spokane	0.49	0.9%	0.79	21.9%	9.0%	0.90	6.7%	82.0%	0.79	2.6%	2.5%	97.4%	102.5%	0.7	1.3	0.8	1.0	0.7
St. Louis	2.86	0.2%	-0.30	19.9%	5.8%	0.89	8.6%	91.0%	0.95	8.8%	2.5%	98.6%	103.5%	0.9	1.1	1.6	1.2	0.9
Tacoma	0.83	0.7%	0.50	22.3%	9.0%	0.73	14.0%	89.0%	0.87	3.7%	2.9%	99.7%	106.1%	0.5	1.2	1.0	1.1	0.6
Tampa/St. Petersburg	2.93	1.1%	9.28	18.6%	10.3%	0.81	9.7%	95.0%	0.87	11.0%	3.1%	98.6%	105.6%	1.1	1.0	0.5	0.8	1.1
Tucson	1.03	2.7%	6.83	20.8%	18.0%	0.74	9.3%	92.0%	0.77	8.6%	3.5%	95.4%	103.8%	0.8	1.1	0.2	0.9	0.8
Virginia Beach/Norfolk	1.73	0.6%	0.46	24.2%	8.7%	0.96	7.2%	91.0%	0.89	7.9%	2.0%	97.0%	101.1%	0.8	0.9	0.4	1.0	0.8
Washington, DC—District	0.67	1.4%	0.72	33.2%	17.7%	1.29	4.2%	117.0%	1.61	21.7%	1.9%	104.9%	109.3%	1.3	1.1	0.0	0.0	2.2
Washington, DC—MD suburbs	0.49	0.6%	0.17	18.2%	9.1%	0.73	5.5%	110.0%	1.09	20.3%	1.5%	100.2%	104.0%	0.8	0.9	0.6	0.3	0.9
Washington, DC—Northern VA	2.97	1.5%	3.55	21.4%	12.8%	1.08	5.1%	110.0%	1.37	18.8%	2.2%	103.9%	110.5%	1.7	0.7	0.2	0.1	1.6
Westchester/Fairfield, NY/CT	1.92	0.2%	-0.96	17.4%	7.1%	1.22	9.4%	120%	1.74	20.7%	2.1%	98.6%	103.4%	1.0	1.2	0.7	0.5	1.1

Table 3-2 Housing

Market	Households		Median Home Prices				2015 Single-Family Home Year-to-Year Change					Multifamily Metrics		
	2015 total (000s)	3-year projected growth	2015 price	2014–2015 % change	2015 as % of peak	Affordability index*	Permits	Starts	Completions	Sales	Walk Score	Rent/cost of ownership**	Rent as % of household income	Space under construction as % of inventory
United States	**122,587**	**3.0%**	**$278,841**	**5.4%**	**96.1%**	**157.58**	**53.1%**	**47.0%**	**16.7%**	**15.5%**	**51**	**0.6**	**21.3%**	**3.6%**
Albuquerque	350.99	0.5%	180.468	2.7%	90.9%	153.44	41.1%	33.3%	10.0%	10.8%	40	0.6	18.6%	3.8%
Atlanta	2,096.57	4.2%	$161,733	6.1%	94.4%	213.92	-58.4%	-62.3%	-58.8%	20.6%	46	0.7	17.2%	2.4%
Austin	758.08	6.0%	$242,285	3.3%	128.4%	154.24	43.6%	40.1%	11.5%	13.3%	35	0.5	18.0%	9.1%
Baltimore	1,082.97	2.7%	$261,122	5.3%	91.7%	168.31	32.2%	24.2%	-6.0%	-0.8%	66	0.6	18.6%	4.8%
Birmingham	461.02	2.4%	$174,111	4.2%	105.5%	168.13	-0.8%	-0.9%	-1.8%	5.8%	33	0.6	18.8%	2.0%
Boise	249.20	4.1%	$177,250	5.6%	86.1%	169.12	46.7%	35.2%	-6.3%	25.3%	37	0.6	17.2%	1.3%
Boston	1,854.54	2.9%	$412,421	4.9%	101.0%	125.54	47.2%	42.2%	23.5%	12.5%	80	0.6	29.5%	4.7%
Buffalo	469.56	0.5%	$139,998	3.7%	126.0%	251.19	71.2%	63.8%	26.8%	13.7%	65	0.8	18.0%	2.0%
Cape Coral/Fort Myers/Naples	444.13	6.8%	$328,713	4.7%	84.4%	108.77	69.5%	58.6%	13.9%	16.1%	36	0.4	21.0%	1.0%
Charleston	284.79	4.1%	$240,811	9.6%	112.1%	123.49	9.2%	1.6%	-24.2%	18.7%	34	0.5	19.7%	6.8%
Charlotte	761.18	6.1%	$183,676	6.1%	117.7%	176.87	14.6%	7.2%	-14.4%	10.8%	24	0.6	17.6%	9.1%
Chicago	3,577.31	1.4%	$200,395	5.7%	73.3%	182.31	23.6%	20.2%	16.9%	12.2%	75	0.8	21.4%	1.9%
Cincinnati	861.94	2.1%	$135,512	1.3%	93.3%	247.18	46.1%	45.2%	14.5%	16.9%	50	0.8	16.6%	1.8%
Cleveland	838.67	0.3%	$120,226	3.7%	86.4%	263.99	80.0%	82.0%	33.8%	12.7%	57	0.9	18.1%	1.5%
Columbia	323.70	4.5%	$149,636	2.4%	102.3%	200.78	30.9%	26.1%	4.2%	12.1%	35	0.7	18.6%	4.3%
Columbus	762.13	2.5%	$151,746	8.1%	101.2%	220.34	20.5%	19.9%	-5.9%	13.8%	40	0.7	15.7%	3.8%
Dallas/Fort Worth	2,580.90	5.1%	$182,124	5.2%	122.1%	184.91	65.3%	59.5%	25.4%	13.7%	44	0.6	16.0%	3.8%
Deltona/Daytona	225.73	5.0%	$131,943	11.7%	64.2%	182.78	73.2%	55.7%	-2.9%	13.3%	13	0.9	23.2%	0.0%
Denver	1,124.02	4.3%	$298,464	7.2%	119.6%	127.70	46.3%	38.1%	14.0%	15.5%	56	0.4	17.6%	6.5%
Des Moines	235.92	1.7%	$170,758	1.3%	112.1%	207.88	43.6%	44.4%	14.1%	22.3%	42	0.7	15.9%	4.4%
Detroit	1,695.75	1.2%	$81,382	8.4%	50.4%	426.23	58.2%	47.5%	-8.2%	20.6%	52	1.5	18.9%	0.6%
Fort Lauderdale	720.09	4.0%	$268,804	13.3%	73.3%	112.86	121.0%	103.1%	11.4%	31.1%	54	0.6	26.9%	4.9%
Greenville	267.72	3.7%	$166,756	5.3%	107.8%	166.06	-54.9%	-62.4%	-73.0%	14.5%	41	0.6	17.2%	0.8%
Hartford	478.67	1.4%	$231,560	3.5%	88.2%	187.30	98.9%	91.1%	13.4%	28.1%	68	0.6	17.5%	4.0%
Honolulu	327.43	2.5%	$700,472	6.3%	109.5%	60.48	66.3%	61.0%	44.9%	23.4%	63	0.3	21.5%	0.0%
Houston	2,305.94	4.3%	$193,291	7.2%	127.1%	169.22	21.2%	18.1%	0.1%	9.6%	44	0.6	16.7%	4.2%
Indianapolis	732.24	3.0%	$145,930	7.8%	118.6%	229.83	62.6%	62.8%	26.8%	10.2%	29	0.7	15.6%	2.9%
Inland Empire	1,403.82	3.7%	$270,893	11.9%	67.5%	110.90	121.2%	105.5%	30.9%	15.3%	39	0.6	23.6%	1.3%
Jacksonville	559.03	4.0%	$171,398	4.9%	89.0%	179.78	33.3%	24.7%	-9.2%	13.5%	26	0.7	18.6%	2.2%
Kansas City, MO	845.10	2.5%	$157,767	3.4%	101.7%	221.91	42.5%	35.4%	-7.3%	8.9%	32	0.7	15.0%	4.4%
Las Vegas	790.11	5.5%	$194,555	12.1%	61.4%	147.79	35.4%	25.6%	-15.7%	17.2%	39	0.6	19.4%	1.1%
Los Angeles	3,392.94	2.2%	$436,424	9.9%	78.1%	72.08	39.9%	29.5%	8.1%	23.7%	50	0.5	31.2%	2.2%
Louisville	534.36	1.6%	$141,072	1.5%	102.8%	220.87	31.1%	19.6%	-25.0%	10.9%	31	0.7	16.5%	3.2%
Madison	249.24	3.0%	$225,659	4.3%	99.6%	170.10	74.6%	71.7%	31.6%	13.9%	47	0.6	17.1%	4.0%
Memphis	520.29	2.5%	$140,083	10.1%	98.6%	193.39	80.0%	80.9%	56.4%	15.0%	33	0.7	18.3%	2.5%
Miami	908.22	3.6%	$258,434	10.1%	68.4%	93.61	107.8%	102.0%	45.0%	67.5%	76	0.6	30.5%	7.4%
Milwaukee	636.07	1.4%	$204,636	3.3%	92.9%	166.01	74.0%	74.1%	22.7%	15.4%	59	0.6	19.1%	1.8%
Minneapolis/St. Paul	1,371.25	2.9%	$203,649	5.2%	87.6%	197.31	75.0%	77.1%	46.6%	18.2%	65	0.7	18.0%	3.3%

Sources: U.S. Census Bureau, Moody's Analytics, WalkScore, U.S. Federal Reserve, Reis, CoStar, and Bureau of Economic Analysis.

* Affordability is the percentage of the median price home that can be purchased with the median income for the market.

** Market apartment rent/median mortgage payment, taxes, insurance, and maintenance.

Table 3-2 Housing

Market	Households 2015 total (000s)	Households 3-year projected growth	Median Home Prices 2015 price	Median Home Prices 2014–2015 % change	Median Home Prices 2015 as % of peak	Median Home Prices Affordability index*	2015 Single-Family Home Year-to-Year Change Permits	Starts	Completions	Sales	Walk Score	Multifamily Metrics Rent/cost of ownership**	Rent as % of household income	Space under construction as % of inventory
United States	**122,587**	**3.0%**	**$278,841**	**5.4%**	**96.1%**	**157.58**	**53.1%**	**47.0%**	**16.7%**	**15.5%**	**51**	**0.6**	**21.3%**	**3.6%**
Nashville	669.28	2.5%	$175,378	3.4%	95.9%	186.63	48.3%	46.3%	37.7%	22.8%	26	0.7	17.5%	7.6%
New Orleans	472.13	1.9%	$168,142	2.5%	97.5%	166.87	49.5%	52.8%	58.4%	11.0%	56	0.8	22.2%	4.2%
New York—Brooklyn	943.54	2.0%	$420,320	4.1%	92.0%	60.17	64.6%	54.7%	90.0%	14.1%	97	0.8	56.2%	2.2%
New York—other boroughs	2,410.22	1.4%	$492,093	0.0%	105.0%	87.62	74.9%	70.0%	36.3%	14.2%	83	0.6	38.9%	1.0%
New York—Manhattan	781.18	1.0%	$464,019	5.6%	93.7%	30.99	63.8%	53.9%	90.1%	19.0%	100	1.0	50.6%	1.6%
Northern New Jersey	778.38	1.0%	$414,949	6.8%	93.7%	116.74	55.3%	55.3%	59.1%	15.0%	78	0.6	25.1%	5.0%
Oakland/East Bay	966.15	2.0%	$755,231	6.2%	98.0%	64.60	67.1%	58.2%	26.1%	15.9%	69	0.3	22.8%	2.0%
Oklahoma City	528.66	3.5%	$162,353	3.5%	116.0%	194.05	12.4%	8.3%	-9.3%	14.3%	32	0.5	13.9%	2.8%
Omaha	357.33	3.9%	$157,073	5.1%	113.7%	220.62	50.5%	50.2%	15.4%	9.2%	41	0.7	15.9%	4.7%
Orange County	1,045.20	2.5%	$727,073	4.3%	102.7%	62.25	48.5%	40.8%	14.3%	15.1%	51	0.3	25.9%	3.3%
Orlando	881.76	6.0%	$192,224	5.2%	71.5%	154.63	48.1%	39.3%	3.3%	10.1%	39	0.7	21.7%	5.2%
Palm Beach	568.60	4.9%	$286,395	5.8%	73.0%	115.69	70.9%	61.3%	21.4%	12.0%	40	0.6	26.4%	3.6%
Philadelphia	2,313.43	1.6%	$239,327	7.3%	102.6%	173.31	81.3%	74.0%	19.8%	19.5%	77	0.7	20.8%	3.0%
Phoenix	1,703.32	5.6%	$214,741	7.0%	80.4%	152.63	84.5%	81.2%	69.1%	19.9%	52	0.5	16.2%	3.5%
Pittsburgh	1,020.94	1.3%	$145,591	5.5%	122.1%	241.10	57.8%	54.1%	13.2%	18.4%	60	0.9	20.5%	3.1%
Portland, ME	221.87	1.6%	$239,929	4.2%	98.2%	147.69	56.8%	51.1%	-7.3%	16.5%	57	0.7	23.1%	0.8%
Portland, OR	946.70	3.3%	$298,633	5.1%	101.4%	126.05	67.5%	62.0%	33.9%	17.6%	63	0.4	18.2%	4.1%
Providence	626.18	1.2%	$244,909	5.4%	83.8%	149.25	82.7%	81.0%	39.4%	15.4%	76	0.7	26.3%	1.6%
Raleigh/Durham	911.88	4.5%	$215,521	0.0%	116.0%	181.57	20.4%	14.5%	-8.6%	11.5%	29	0.5	16.2%	8.0%
Richmond	518.93	2.7%	$253,454	3.6%	108.8%	137.63	94.2%	89.3%	43.2%	16.7%	49	0.5	18.1%	3.8%
Sacramento	828.87	2.7%	$275,274	5.6%	73.5%	137.49	106.3%	95.3%	42.2%	14.9%	33	0.5	18.9%	3.2%
Salt Lake City	401.77	3.1%	$264,633	4.0%	114.2%	136.18	54.6%	50.6%	24.0%	10.2%	55	0.4	14.7%	4.1%
San Antonio	852.25	4.5%	$185,380	3.7%	121.2%	166.41	68.9%	65.3%	28.3%	12.2%	34	0.6	18.0%	4.7%
San Diego	1,149.76	2.3%	$523,015	5.3%	86.8%	73.41	96.6%	88.6%	49.0%	15.0%	49	0.4	26.1%	2.5%
San Francisco	743.59	2.7%	$1,084,748	2.8%	114.8%	49.68	54.8%	48.8%	28.7%	10.4%	84	0.3	30.8%	7.4%
San Jose	649.42	2.2%	$890,417	3.7%	106.5%	64.06	43.9%	42.6%	37.4%	12.7%	48	0.3	20.0%	6.5%
Seattle	1,139.35	3.5%	$411,774	4.4%	98.0%	110.62	28.6%	10.9%	-30.0%	8.5%	71	0.4	19.4%	5.3%
Spokane	198.37	3.0%	$189,920	6.0%	97.4%	170.44	34.9%	12.9%	-38.7%	8.8%	36	0.5	18.5%	0.6%
St. Louis	1,163.62	1.6%	$145,796	4.4%	99.1%	241.88	60.8%	59.0%	16.1%	13.0%	60	0.7	16.6%	0.7%
Tacoma	317.18	2.7%	$226,015	4.1%	84.1%	156.70	14.8%	-9.5%	-52.3%	12.6%	51	0.5	17.4%	1.9%
Tampa/St. Petersburg	1,200.19	3.1%	$165,987	8.2%	73.6%	182.61	58.6%	56.0%	39.6%	7.6%	46	0.8	22.6%	2.5%
Tucson	411.61	6.3%	$194,163	7.0%	79.3%	151.77	82.9%	82.8%	77.1%	13.0%	39	0.5	17.4%	0.6%
Virginia Beach/Norfolk	656.76	2.3%	$196,236	3.6%	80.5%	169.90	79.9%	77.4%	52.3%	16.3%	38	0.7	21.5%	5.4%
Washington, DC—District	289.60	2.8%	$383,158	3.0%	102.4%	110.97	-11.7%	-20.8%	-82.1%	8.4%	74	0.6	26.9%	6.1%
Washington, DC—MD suburbs	173.78	2.1%	$365,400	4.6%	91.8%	134.12	60.6%	55.2%	26.1%	16.1%	47	0.5	19.1%	5.8%
Washington, DC—Northern VA	1,077.23	3.9%	$376,260	4.0%	91.3%	131.98	83.6%	81.3%	52.1%	20.6%	56	0.6	23.6%	6.1%
Westchester/Fairfield, NY/CT	696.18	1.3%	$531,422	7.0%	89.8%	103.86	33.2%	28.2%	46.4%	17.9%	51	0.5	27.3%	9.5%

Boston (9). Boston remains in the top ten of this year's survey. Boston is also the highest-ranked Northeast region market. Interviewees were attracted to how well the entrenched higher education infrastructure in Boston continues to provide the market with a young and well-trained workforce. In addition, the growing life sciences industry continues to grow in targeted locations within the Boston market.

Coming in at number five, the hotel sector is the highest-ranked property type in Boston. The retail sector also is highly ranked in Boston at number eight. The office sector in Boston remains attractive to investors, and survey respondents put it at number 11 for 2015. Survey expectations for 2015 are a little less positive in regard to the Boston housing market, with the single-family sector coming in at number 14 and the multifamily sector coming in at number 21. The results of the survey put the industrial sector at number 26.

Boston is no different than the other major core markets and will continue to attract significant amounts of institutional capital. This is reflected by the input from local market participants who view investor demand and the availability of capital as the strongest components of the Boston real estate market. This interest

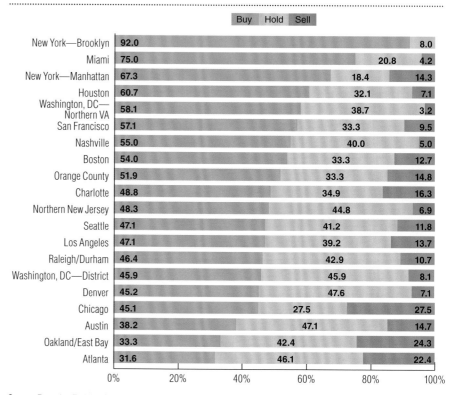

Exhibit 3-10 U.S. Retail Property Buy/Hold/Sell Recommendations

	Buy	Hold	Sell
New York—Brooklyn	92.0		8.0
Miami	75.0	20.8	4.2
New York—Manhattan	67.3	18.4	14.3
Houston	60.7	32.1	7.1
Washington, DC—Northern VA	58.1	38.7	3.2
San Francisco	57.1	33.3	9.5
Nashville	55.0	40.0	5.0
Boston	54.0	33.3	12.7
Orange County	51.9	33.3	14.8
Charlotte	48.8	34.9	16.3
Northern New Jersey	48.3	44.8	6.9
Seattle	47.1	41.2	11.8
Los Angeles	47.1	39.2	13.7
Raleigh/Durham	46.4	42.9	10.7
Washington, DC—District	45.9	45.9	8.1
Denver	45.2	47.6	7.1
Chicago	45.1	27.5	27.5
Austin	38.2	47.1	14.7
Oakland/East Bay	33.3	42.4	24.3
Atlanta	31.6	46.1	22.4

Source: *Emerging Trends in Real Estate 2015* survey.

Note: Cities listed are the top 20 rated for investment in the retail sector; in this exhibit, cities are ordered according to the number of "buy" recommendations.

is likely justified, as the local market also feels good about the strength of the local economy.

Raleigh/Durham (10). Raleigh/Durham rounds out the top ten markets in this year's survey. Interviewees expressed interest in Raleigh/Durham due to the attractiveness of the market to the millennial generation along with a number of projects that are enhancing the urbanization of Raleigh/Durham. This activity is creating an environment that is conducive to attracting and retaining a high-quality workforce. In addition to a highly qualified labor force, Raleigh/Durham offers companies a very competitive cost of doing business.

The trend toward a more urbanized feel has survey respondents feeling positive

about the Raleigh/Durham office market, and it is ranked number seven. The appeal of the market to future residents is being reflected in a single-family housing ranking of number nine and a retail ranking of 13. The industrial sector in Raleigh/Durham has historically been skewed toward higher-finish product that has been designed to serve the local technology industries. Survey respondents feel relatively good about the industrial market in Raleigh/Durham, and it is currently ranked number 15. The multifamily ranking for the market is just outside the top one-third of markets at number 29. The lower ranking may reflect the relative affordability of single-family housing. The hotel sector is the lowest-ranked property type in Raleigh/Durham for 2015.

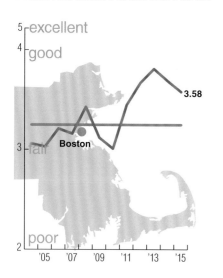

5 — excellent
4 — good
3.58
Boston
3 — fair
poor
2
'05 '07 '09 '11 '13 '15

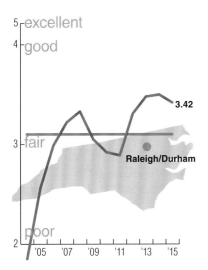

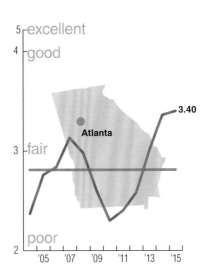

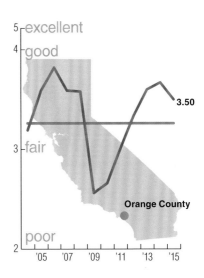

Raleigh/Durham is more of an emerging market in terms of institutional interest, and capital flowing to the market is expected to continue to increase. The market does, however, have a very strong local property owner community. Local market participants feel that the strength of the local economy will drive activity in 2015. The continued strength of the economy could provide investment opportunities for a growing institutional investor base as well as support the strong local development community.

Atlanta (11). The economic recovery and size of the Atlanta real estate market led survey respondents to rank Atlanta as the number-11 market in this year's survey. The diverse economy, low cost of doing business, and affordable housing resulted in all six property sectors being ranked in the top one-third of the markets in the survey.

Survey respondents placed all of the Atlanta property sectors in the top one-third of all the markets surveyed. Atlanta's affordable single-family market was viewed as attractive, resulting in a housing sector rank of number ten. The other property sectors with ranks in the top 20 are multifamily (number 15), hotel (number 17), industrial (number 18), and

office (number 20). The retail sector has the lowest rank at number 23.

The Atlanta market is attractive to institutional and local investors and developers. Local market participants assess the availability of capital and strong local development community as two of the best attributes of the Atlanta market. Confidence in the strength of the local economy and expected investor demand could drive real estate activity in 2015.

Orange County, California (12). Orange County joins Los Angeles to become the second southern California market in this year's top 20. The Orange County economy has bounced back from being the epicenter of the subprime mortgage collapse. The recovery in financial services, technology-related employment, and a strong import/export component have led the recovery in the Orange County economy.

Survey respondents placed the majority of the Orange County property sectors in the top 20 by property type. The industrial sector, which is composed of smaller properties, ranked ninth. Other property sectors that placed well in this year's survey include office and single-family housing at number 15, retail at number

16, and multifamily at number 19. The only property sector outside the top one-third is hotel at number 31.

As part of the larger southern California metro areas, Orange County is a market that is appealing to institutional investors. Local market participants feel that investor demand, along with plenty of available capital, will drive the market in 2015. This activity may also be enhanced by the strength of the local economy.

Nashville (13). Nashville continues to be popular with interviewees and survey respondents alike. Interviewees were quick to point out the development in the urban center that is bringing employers and employees together in a vibrant environment. Nashville is attractive to the millennial generation due to its postsecondary education system and entertainment district. The lower cost of doing business has a diverse set of industries expanding in Nashville.

According to the survey results, the Nashville housing market could be one of the best opportunities in 2015. The multi-family sector is ranked number six, while the single-family housing market is ranked number 13. The other Nashville property sectors ranked in the top 20 include hotel

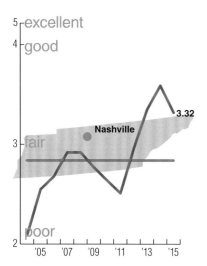

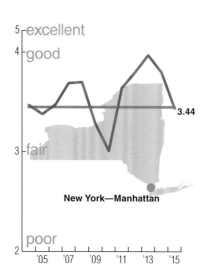

at number 14, office at number 18, and retail at number 19. At number 29, the industrial sector is the only property type falling outside the top one-third.

Historically, the Nashville market has been dominated by local owners and developers. This appears to be changing as institutional investors have discovered the improving economy and opportunities offered by growth in the urban center and the increase in the city's industrial base. Local perceptions of the market are that the strength in the local economy will continue to drive investor demand in 2015. The increasing interest in the market by national institutional investors will be supported by the strong local development community.

New York—Manhattan (14). Manhattan slips out of the top ten in this year's survey, but the decline may well be due to its own success. Manhattan is clearly one of the major markets that have recovered from the recession. Manhattan is a classic example of a city where global investors feel confident investing in real estate, knowing their capital will be safe. This has led to an influx of global capital to the market in all property types, ultimately making the size of many transactions out of reach for some domestic

investors. Manhattan remains the financial center of the United States, but much of the economic growth can be attributed to a growing technology center further enhancing the diversity of the economy.

Manhattan is expensive, but if you have the capital, survey respondents feel there may be good investment opportunities. The survey results put retail at number three, hotel at number nine, office at number ten, and multifamily at number 13 as the best options for 2015. The industrial and single-family housing sectors are viewed somewhat less favorably and are ranked in the bottom one-third, as both are ranked number 53 for 2015.

Manhattan is clearly the most attractive destination for global and domestic capital in the United States. This isn't likely to change in 2015 as strength in the local economy and investor demand should keep the market active in 2015. A unique strength of the Manhattan market has been the cooperation between public and private groups to make some of the massive real estate projects undertaken in the city a reality.

San Jose (15). San Jose becomes the second Bay Area market in the top 20. It is all about technology in San Jose, but

instead of semiconductors and microprocessors, more of the growth is driven by mobile computing and social media. It is unlikely that San Jose will be unseated as the technology center of the United States any time soon, but it does face challenges since today's workforce requires a more urban feel. The car-centric San Jose area has been making adjustments. Companies have required the development of new or redevelopment of existing space and have started new transportation plans that allow workers to live in San Francisco's more urban environment.

The survey results reveal a somewhat bifurcated San Jose market. Respondents put the multifamily, office, and housing sectors at the top of the survey. The industrial, retail, and hotel property types are somewhat lower, in the middle one-third of the markets surveyed. At number five, the multifamily sector is the highest-ranked San Jose property type, followed by office at number eight and single-family housing at number 11. The industrial sector is ranked at number 31, retail at number 36, and hotel at number 40.

The strength of the technology industry and the support industries it requires have made San Jose attractive to institutional investors. The size and diversity of the

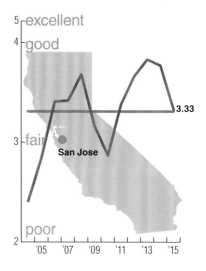

Exhibit 3-11 U.S. Hotel Property Buy/Hold/Sell Recommendations

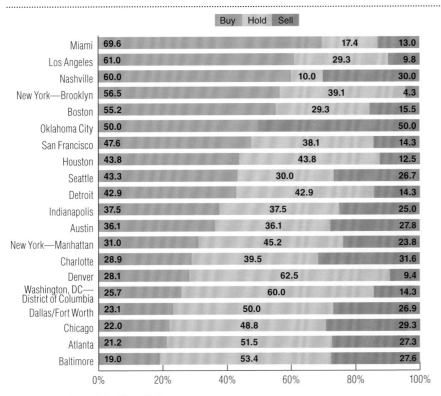

	Buy	Hold	Sell
Miami	69.6	17.4	13.0
Los Angeles	61.0	29.3	9.8
Nashville	60.0	10.0	30.0
New York—Brooklyn	56.5	39.1	4.3
Boston	55.2	29.3	15.5
Oklahoma City	50.0		50.0
San Francisco	47.6	38.1	14.3
Houston	43.8	43.8	12.5
Seattle	43.3	30.0	26.7
Detroit	42.9	42.9	14.3
Indianapolis	37.5	37.5	25.0
Austin	36.1	36.1	27.8
New York—Manhattan	31.0	45.2	23.8
Charlotte	28.9	39.5	31.6
Denver	28.1	62.5	9.4
Washington, DC— District of Columbia	25.7	60.0	14.3
Dallas/Fort Worth	23.1	50.0	26.9
Chicago	22.0	48.8	29.3
Atlanta	21.2	51.5	27.3
Baltimore	19.0	53.4	27.6

0%   20%   40%   60%   80%   100%

Source: *Emerging Trends in Real Estate 2015* survey.

Note: Cities listed are the top 20 rated for investment in the hotel sector; in this exhibit, cities are ordered according to the number of "buy" recommendations.

market also offer opportunities for local owners and developers. Local market participants see the strength of the local economy driving strong investor demand in 2015. This demand should be accommodated by the availability of capital. The need to make some older properties meet new workforce requirements is also seen as providing good opportunities for redevelopment investments.

Portland, Oregon (16). Portland remains in the top 20 in 2015 based largely on its attraction to the millennial generation, steps it has taken to create a vibrant urban core, and a diverse economy that has components from manufacturing, technology, and warehousing and distribution. Portland is a classic example of a market where population growth may lead employment growth. The market

is appealing enough to the millennial generation that they are likely to move there without the guarantee of permanent employment. As this base of workers builds, it is possible that companies will choose to relocate to tap into this attractive pool of labor.

Expected strength in the housing market supports Portland's position in the top 20 this year. Survey respondents ranked the multifamily sector at number four and the single-family sector at number eight. At number 21, the industrial sector is the only other property type in the top one-third. The remaining property types are office and hotel at number 30 and retail at number 48.

The Portland real estate market supports a wide range of real estate players,

includes an active real estate services industry, and is attractive to institutional and local owners and developers. Local market participants see the strength of the local economy as the driving force for 2015. Capital is expected to be readily available, so this should support a healthy level of investor demand. One potential drawback seen in the market may be fewer development or redevelopment opportunities in the market.

Oakland/East Bay (17). Oakland joins San Francisco and San Jose in the top 20 this year to complete the Bay Area sweep. Oakland typically benefits as a lower-cost base of operations when business costs in the San Francisco market no longer make economic sense for a company. Oakland also benefits as a more affordable housing market for San Francisco. The strength of the San Francisco economy, along with the diverse labor force in Oakland, may be behind survey respondents' confidence in the market.

Survey respondents ranked the Oakland multifamily sector in the top ten at number seven for 2015. The office sector, at number 13, and industrial property, at number 14, are also expected to be good investment options for the coming year. Retail

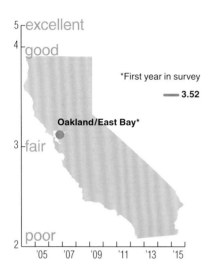

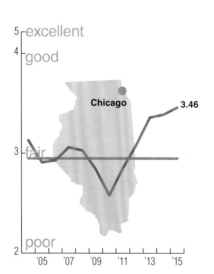

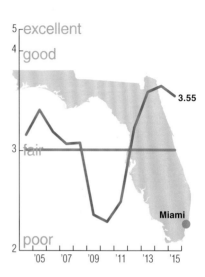

at number 21, single-family housing at number 24, and hotel at number 48 round out survey expectation results.

Oakland's location in the Bay Area makes it a viable option for institutional investors. Despite this, being a location outside the San Francisco core also offers a number of opportunities for local owners and developers. Local Oakland market participants see the local economy as being strong in 2015. The economy is expected to support strong investor demand that is supported by the availability of capital.

Chicago (18). Chicago represents the only market from the Midwest region in this year's top 20. Interviewees expressed concern about the fiscal situation surrounding the city of Chicago, but the fact that the city is still one of the largest urban cores in the United States has led to a continued flow of capital into the market. Chicago still has one of the most diverse economic bases in the country, and is positioned to see stronger economic growth as manufacturing activity in the Midwest improves and will benefit if energy prices continue to decline.

The industrial and multifamily property types were the highest-ranked Chicago property types, with both coming in at number eight in the 2015 survey. Survey

respondents also placed the retail sector at number 18 and hotel at number 20 near the top of the survey. The office sector, ranked number 26, and single-family housing, at 28, round out the expectations for Chicago.

Chicago is one of the major core real estate markets in the United States and as such is very appealing to both domestic and global real estate investors. The opinion of the local market participants is that capital will be available for investments in the market and that investor demand will remain strong despite some concern over the strength of the local economy. One area where local participants may want some improvement is in the area of the public and private sectors working together to improve the local market.

Miami (19). Miami appears in the top 20 again for the second year in a row. Survey respondents obviously feel that the market has fully recovered from the housing bust meltdown that had many thinking it would be years before the market returned to more normalized conditions. Miami is one of the original "hedge cities"—i.e., cities where foreign investors like to set up a second base of operations. Miami has long served this purpose

for Latin America, but the sharp decline in housing prices during the downturn made Miami attractive to investors from around the world. The result is that the construction market is up and running again in Miami and that is driving growth in a number of support industries.

The Miami property types favored by survey respondents are retail at number nine, hotel at number ten, and office and multifamily—both at number 16 in the respective property type rankings. Industrial, at number 34, and single-family housing, at number 40, complete the survey expectations for Miami property types.

The flow of global capital into Miami actually helped the market recover from the economic downturn. Now that the market has recovered, there is no reason to believe that global and domestic investors will find the market any less appealing. Local Miami participants are very positive on the market, feeling that investor demand and the strength of the local economy will support strong activity in 2015.

San Diego (20). San Diego rounds out the top 20 in the 2015 survey, bringing the number of West Coast markets in the top 20 to eight and the sixth market in

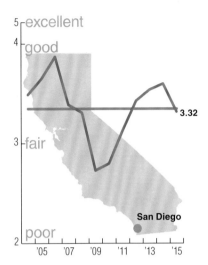

California. Survey respondents and interviewees like the well-educated workforce, technology industry exposure, and growing millennial population that San Diego has to offer.

The San Diego housing sector is viewed as offering one of the best opportunities in 2015 by this year's survey respondents. The results of the survey show the San Diego multifamily sector ranked number 11 and the single-family sector ranked number 16. At number 19, the San Diego office sector is the only other property type ranked in the top 20. The survey results place the hotel sector at number 33, retail at number 35, and industrial at number 38.

San Diego is a smaller market on the West Coast, but the industrial base keeps it on the radar of a large number of institutional investors. The local owner/ development community also remains very active in the market. Survey participants with the most knowledge about the San Diego market see investor demand as a strong suit for 2015. The strength of the local economy and the availability of capital are expected to support the level of investor interest.

Perspective on Regions

Midwest Region

The 13 markets that constitute the Midwest region have an average survey rank of 44, with Chicago leading the way at number 18. The next-highest-ranked markets in the region are Indianapolis, Minneapolis/St. Paul, and Kansas City.

The industrial and multifamily sectors are expected to offer the best potential for 2015 in the Midwest region. Survey respondents see the hotel property type and housing market as offering fair investment opportunities in the coming year. The office and retail sectors are viewed as being the most challenged in the region.

The Midwest industrial market has experienced improvement due to the increase in demand for goods and services from local economies and increased industrial production in the region. Survey respondents have ranked the potential for industrial as good in Chicago, Indianapolis, Minneapolis/St. Paul, Kansas City, and Cincinnati. The expectations for Detroit, Columbus, and Des Moines are also favorable.

The multifamily sector has benefited from comparatively low levels of new supply while household growth has been steady.

Table 3-3 Midwest Region: Sector and Local Outlook Scores

Overall Rank		Investment Prospect Scores, by Sector						Local outlook score*
		Office	Retail	Industrial	Multifamily	Hotel	Housing	
18	Chicago	2.96	3.24	3.76	3.87	3.07	3.08	3.70
24	Indianapolis	2.99	2.83	3.51	3.49	3.16	3.10	3.97
30	Minneapolis/St. Paul	2.79	2.75	3.37	3.30	3.02	3.08	4.06
33	Kansas City, MO	2.71	2.68	3.29	3.08	2.72	3.28	3.74
37	Columbus	2.93	2.98	3.13	3.08	2.69	3.01	3.88
38	Detroit	2.54	2.77	3.19	3.34	3.19	2.87	3.51
41	St. Louis	2.87	2.63	2.98	3.05	2.69	2.98	3.23
52	Cleveland	2.55	2.36	2.88	3.06	2.81	2.76	3.36
53	Madison	2.83	2.76	2.55	2.98	2.98	2.55	3.85
54	Cincinnati	2.18	2.19	3.25	3.26	2.62	2.76	3.49
57	Des Moines	2.41	2.44	3.08	2.98	3.00	2.55	3.53
61	Omaha	2.55	2.97	2.34	2.55	2.55	2.55	3.75
71	Milwaukee	2.49	2.79	2.76	2.98	2.34	1.84	3.32
44	**Midwest average**	**2.68**	**2.72**	**3.08**	**3.15**	**2.83**	**2.80**	**3.65**

Source: *Emerging Trends in Real Estate 2015* survey.

*Average score of local market participants' opinion on strength of local economy, investor demand, capital availability, development and redevelopment opportunities, public/private investments, and local development community.

Exhibit 3-12 Local Outlook: Midwest Region

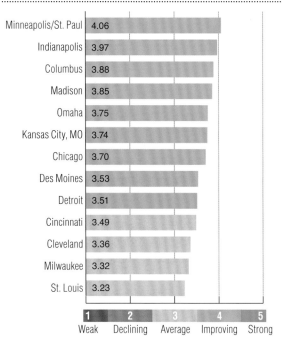

Minneapolis/St. Paul	4.06
Indianapolis	3.97
Columbus	3.88
Madison	3.85
Omaha	3.75
Kansas City, MO	3.74
Chicago	3.70
Des Moines	3.53
Detroit	3.51
Cincinnati	3.49
Cleveland	3.36
Milwaukee	3.32
St. Louis	3.23

1	2	3	4	5
Weak	Declining	Average	Improving	Strong

Source: *Emerging Trends in Real Estate 2015* survey.

Note: Average score of local market participants' opinion on strength of local economy, investor demand, capital availability, development and redevelopment opportunities, public/private investments, and local development community.

Multifamily investment prospects are considered good for Chicago, Indianapolis, Minneapolis/St. Paul, Detroit, and Cincinnati. The expectations for Cleveland, St. Louis, Madison, Des Moines, and Milwaukee are not far behind.

The lack of hotel development in the region during the economic downturn and the upturn in local economic growth have survey respondents expecting the hotel sector to be at least an average performer in the Midwest region in 2015. Detroit, Indianapolis, Chicago, and Des Moines have the highest scores in the sector.

The Midwest housing sector is a somewhat mixed picture. Survey respondents have a positive outlook for Kansas City, Indianapolis, Chicago, and Minneapolis/St. Paul. The expectations, however, are lower for Milwaukee, Omaha, Des Moines, and Madison.

Survey respondents perceive the office sector as the weakest property type in the Midwest. The regional average score is only fair, with Indianapolis and Chicago selected as having the best potential for 2015.

Local Midwest market participants view the market conditions as good for 2015. Minneapolis/St. Paul, Indianapolis, Madison,

and Columbus lead the outlook for the region. The expectations for St. Louis, Cleveland, and Milwaukee are still good, but somewhat muted compared with those for the rest of the region.

Northeast Region

The 13 markets that make up the Northeast region have an average 2015 survey rank of 44. The results are somewhat bifurcated, with markets such as Boston (number nine), Manhattan (number 14), and Brooklyn (number 22) all in the top one-third of all markets. The markets from the bottom of survey include Buffalo (number 75), Providence (number 74), and Portland, Maine (number 68).

Survey respondents rank the multifamily and retail sectors as having the best investment potential in the Northeast region. The industrial, single-family housing, and hotel sectors are expected to be slightly below the leading two, but still offer fair investment opportunities. Despite some of the largest office markets in the country being located in the region, office investment opportunities trail the other sectors.

The expectations for the multifamily sector are very good for most of the markets in the Northeast region. The three markets

Exhibit 3-13 Local Outlook: Northeast Region

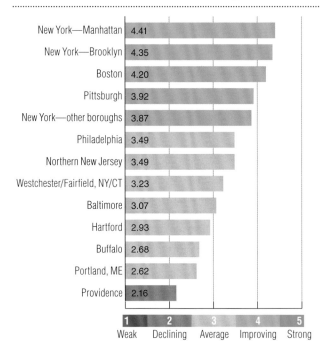

New York—Manhattan	4.41
New York—Brooklyn	4.35
Boston	4.20
Pittsburgh	3.92
New York—other boroughs	3.87
Philadelphia	3.49
Northern New Jersey	3.49
Westchester/Fairfield, NY/CT	3.23
Baltimore	3.07
Hartford	2.93
Buffalo	2.68
Portland, ME	2.62
Providence	2.16

1	2	3	4	5
Weak	Declining	Average	Improving	Strong

Source: *Emerging Trends in Real Estate 2015* survey.

Note: Average score of local market participants' opinion on strength of local economy, investor demand, capital availability, development and redevelopment opportunities, public/private investments, and local development community.

Table 3-4 **Northeast Region: Sector and Local Outlook Scores**

Overall Rank		Investment Prospect Scores, by Sector						Local outlook score*
		Office	Retail	Industrial	Multifamily	Hotel	Housing	
14	New York—Manhattan	3.56	3.66	2.91	3.72	3.33	2.77	4.41
22	New York—Brooklyn	3.59	3.33	2.75	4.15	3.20	3.26	4.35
9	Boston	3.53	3.46	3.22	3.61	3.58	3.39	4.20
43	Pittsburgh	2.74	2.61	2.86	3.00	2.81	3.05	3.92
48	New York—other boroughs	2.57	3.11	2.85	3.20	2.55	2.80	3.87
27	Philadelphia	2.83	3.09	3.35	3.59	2.98	3.00	3.49
32	Northern New Jersey	2.42	3.35	3.76	3.71	2.47	2.80	3.49
60	Westchester/Fairfield, NY/CT	2.22	2.88	2.44	2.88	2.40	2.76	3.23
31	Baltimore	2.63	2.82	3.34	3.58	3.08	2.93	3.07
73	Hartford	2.05	2.36	2.32	2.64	2.20	2.27	2.93
75	Buffalo	1.59	1.97	2.13	2.13	1.74	1.97	2.68
68	Portland, ME	1.85	2.30	2.27	2.68	2.73	2.67	2.62
74	Providence	1.70	2.27	1.75	2.46	2.23	2.55	2.16
44	**Northeast average**	**2.56**	**2.86**	**2.76**	**3.18**	**2.71**	**2.79**	**3.42**

Source: *Emerging Trends in Real Estate 2015* survey.

*Average score of local market participants' opinion on strength of local economy, investor demand, capital availability, development and redevelopment opportunities, public/private investments, and local development community.

that make up the New York City area, along with northern New Jersey, are all expected to offer good investment opportunities in 2015. Boston, Philadelphia, and Baltimore also could offer good investment choices.

The heavily urbanized markets are expected to offer the best retail investment opportunities next year. The New York region including northern New Jersey scored well in this year's survey. Philadelphia and Boston are not far behind and could provide investors with good investment chances.

The single-family housing outlook for the region is similar in a number of markets in the region, with Boston, Brooklyn, and Pittsburgh being scored slightly higher by survey participants. Providence, Hartford, and Buffalo are projected to trail the regional average.

Survey views of the Northeast industrial market are mixed. The outlook is good for northern New Jersey, Philadelphia, and Baltimore. Boston, Pittsburgh, and Manhattan have each scored above the regional average.

The results of the survey reflect some caution in regard to the hotel sector in the Northeast, but Boston, Manhattan, and Brooklyn are given scores well above the regional average. Increasing business and leisure travel will likely drive hotel demand and push up room rates in these business center markets.

Based on survey results, respondents expect the office sector to be the most challenged in 2015. This, like several of the other property types, is a very mixed story. Markets like Manhattan, Brooklyn, and Boston all show scores that would indicate that good opportunities may be found in these markets. Other markets with above-regional-average scores include Philadelphia, Baltimore, and Pittsburgh.

West Region

Eight of the 20 markets in the West region are in this year's top 20, so the region has an impressive average rank of 34. Phoenix, at number 26, is the highest-ranked West region market outside of the top 20. Salt Lake City, at number 36, is the only other West region market in the top half of this year's survey.

In general, survey respondents appear to be positive on all property sectors in the West region. The average outlook is good for the multifamily, industrial, and single-family housing sectors. The outlook for the other property types is fair, with the hotel property type trailing the other sectors.

The Bay Area and southern California markets lead the region in terms of outlook for multifamily investments. Albuquerque, Phoenix, Salt Lake City, and Honolulu also are ranked as offering good investment potential in 2015.

Table 3-5 West Region: Sector and Local Outlook Scores

Overall Rank		Investment Prospect Scores, by Sector						Local outlook score*
		Office	Retail	Industrial	Multifamily	Hotel	Housing	
3	San Francisco	3.81	3.61	3.62	3.98	3.89	3.80	4.54
8	Seattle	3.75	3.52	3.92	3.76	3.62	3.34	4.48
15	San Jose	3.62	2.88	3.16	3.91	2.77	3.50	4.41
4	Denver	3.68	3.55	3.62	3.66	3.49	3.87	4.30
6	Los Angeles	3.43	3.27	3.71	3.84	3.67	3.73	4.11
12	Orange County	3.40	3.28	3.72	3.63	2.90	3.36	4.08
20	San Diego	3.27	2.89	3.05	3.76	2.84	3.36	3.98
17	Oakland/East Bay	3.51	3.17	3.55	3.89	2.65	3.15	3.95
16	Portland	2.93	2.75	3.35	3.92	2.94	3.60	3.88
36	Salt Lake City	2.96	2.64	3.05	3.01	2.62	3.26	3.81
26	Phoenix	3.12	2.82	3.68	3.51	2.67	3.14	3.66
46	Inland Empire	2.45	2.39	3.87	3.23	2.35	2.85	3.64
42	Honolulu	2.48	2.67	2.92	3.04	2.95	3.04	3.63
64	Las Vegas	2.02	2.32	2.78	2.90	2.60	2.58	3.49
58	Boise	2.51	2.55	2.81	2.71	2.55	2.74	3.42
67	Spokane	2.02	2.23	2.81	2.73	2.41	2.55	3.27
62	Tacoma	2.21	2.05	3.23	2.98	2.02	2.72	3.26
66	Sacramento	2.00	2.12	2.49	2.52	2.13	2.94	3.24
65	Tucson	2.27	2.21	2.98	2.76	1.28	2.98	2.70
47	Albuquerque	2.70	2.81	2.88	3.52	2.63	2.75	2.66
34	**West average**	**2.91**	**2.79**	**3.26**	**3.36**	**2.75**	**3.16**	**3.73**

Source: *Emerging Trends in Real Estate 2015* survey.

*Average score of local market participants' opinion on strength of local economy, investor demand, capital availability, development and redevelopment opportunities, public/private investments, and local development community.

The Inland Empire and Phoenix are the top regional industrial markets outside of the top 20. Salt Lake City and Tacoma also have good outlooks for 2015. The higher-ranked markets in the West region all have national or regional distribution characteristics. The remaining markets are dependent on the strength of their local economies to drive industrial demand.

Survey respondents like the single-family housing market in the West region. Salt Lake City and Phoenix have the highest scores for markets that are not included in the overall top 20. No market in the West region has an outlook score below fair for 2015.

The overall outlook for the office sector in the West region is fair. The outlook is substantially stronger in the eight markets that were included in the overall top 20, with Phoenix having the highest score for a market not in that top group.

Survey respondents are less favorable toward the potential for retail investments outside of the markets in the overall top 20.

Phoenix and Albuquerque are the highest-scoring markets, but they are in the fair category.

The best opportunities in the hotel sector appear to be concentrated in the markets in the overall top 20, and even these are limited to a smaller number of markets. San Francisco, Los Angeles, Seattle, and Denver appear to offer the best opportunities for 2015.

South Region

Like the West region, the South region also has eight markets in the top 20 of this year's survey. The regional average rank of 35 is one below that achieved by the West. South region markets just outside the top 20 include Charleston, San Antonio, and Washington, D.C.

Survey respondents expect most property types to offer good investment opportunities in 2015. The housing sector, both multifamily and single-family, is the top-scoring sector in the region.

Exhibit 3-14 Local Outlook: West Region

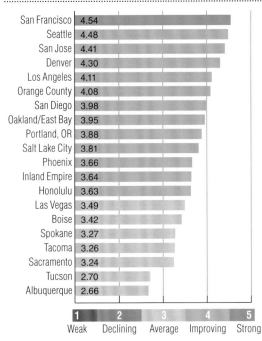

San Francisco	4.54
Seattle	4.48
San Jose	4.41
Denver	4.30
Los Angeles	4.11
Orange County	4.08
San Diego	3.98
Oakland/East Bay	3.95
Portland, OR	3.88
Salt Lake City	3.81
Phoenix	3.66
Inland Empire	3.64
Honolulu	3.63
Las Vegas	3.49
Boise	3.42
Spokane	3.27
Tacoma	3.26
Sacramento	3.24
Tucson	2.70
Albuquerque	2.66

1	2	3	4	5
Weak	Declining	Average	Improving	Strong

Source: *Emerging Trends in Real Estate 2015* survey.

Note: Average score of local market participants' opinion on strength of local economy, investor demand, capital availability, development and redevelopment opportunities, public/private investments, and local development community.

The industrial market also looks attractive in the region, while the retail sector trails the other property types slightly. The hotel and office sectors may be the most challenged in the region, although this will clearly be a market-by-market story.

The expectations for the multifamily sector are responsible for a number of the South region markets making it into the top 20. A number of regional markets outside the top 20 score in the good range as well, including Charleston, Orlando, Palm Beach, San Antonio, and D.C.

Survey results also indicate the expectation that the single-family housing market will do well in 2015. The markets included in the top 20 all score well in the survey. Other markets in the region that scored well in the survey are San Antonio, Charleston, and Greenville.

The industrial market sector scores well in the South region. The combination of secondary port markets along with expanding local economies could create industrial opportunities outside the top 20 markets. Industrial markets outside the top 20 that score well are Tampa/St. Petersburg, Orlando, Jacksonville, Charleston, and Fort Lauderdale.

Exhibit 3-15 Local Outlook: South Region

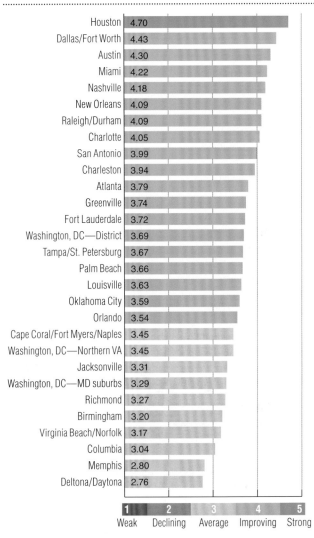

Houston	4.70
Dallas/Fort Worth	4.43
Austin	4.30
Miami	4.22
Nashville	4.18
New Orleans	4.09
Raleigh/Durham	4.09
Charlotte	4.05
San Antonio	3.99
Charleston	3.94
Atlanta	3.79
Greenville	3.74
Fort Lauderdale	3.72
Washington, DC—District	3.69
Tampa/St. Petersburg	3.67
Palm Beach	3.66
Louisville	3.63
Oklahoma City	3.59
Orlando	3.54
Cape Coral/Fort Myers/Naples	3.45
Washington, DC—Northern VA	3.45
Jacksonville	3.31
Washington, DC—MD suburbs	3.29
Richmond	3.27
Birmingham	3.20
Virginia Beach/Norfolk	3.17
Columbia	3.04
Memphis	2.80
Deltona/Daytona	2.76

1	2	3	4	5
Weak	Declining	Average	Improving	Strong

Source: *Emerging Trends in Real Estate 2015* survey.

Note: Average score of local market participants' opinion on strength of local economy, investor demand, capital availability, development and redevelopment opportunities, public/private investments, and local development community.

The retail sector is expected by the survey respondents to offer good opportunities in the South region markets in the top 20. A number of other regional markets also have scores that indicate they could do well in 2015, including New Orleans, San Antonio, and D.C.

The survey reveals the expectation that opportunities for hotel investments are above average in the eight South region markets represented in the top 20. Washington, D.C., is the only regional market outside the top 20 that the survey scores near the good category.

Table 3-6 South Region: Sector and Local Outlook Scores

Overall Rank		Investment Prospect Scores, by Sector						Local outlook score*
		Office	Retail	Industrial	Multifamily	Hotel	Housing	
1	Houston	4.00	3.96	3.97	3.99	3.61	4.21	4.70
5	Dallas/Fort Worth	3.74	2.89	3.84	3.68	3.32	3.98	4.43
2	Austin	4.02	3.80	3.78	3.74	3.50	4.33	4.30
19	Miami	3.39	3.45	3.13	3.68	3.32	2.95	4.22
13	Nashville	3.27	3.17	3.18	3.90	3.16	3.40	4.18
49	New Orleans	2.20	3.33	2.98	2.79	2.82	2.83	4.09
10	Raleigh/Durham	3.63	3.34	3.54	3.42	2.73	3.57	4.09
7	Charlotte	3.51	3.44	3.77	3.49	3.42	3.71	4.05
23	San Antonio	3.13	3.17	2.98	3.19	2.83	3.43	3.99
21	Charleston	3.13	3.10	3.18	3.62	3.04	3.26	3.94
11	Atlanta	3.18	3.14	3.50	3.69	3.11	3.54	3.79
29	Greenville	2.83	2.82	3.53	2.90	2.79	3.26	3.74
44	Fort Lauderdale	2.88	2.92	3.04	3.04	2.63	2.85	3.72
25	Washington, DC—District	2.94	3.39	2.93	3.38	3.09	3.17	3.69
35	Tampa/St. Petersburg	2.55	2.81	3.07	3.17	3.04	3.11	3.67
45	Palm Beach	2.27	2.95	3.00	3.30	2.55	2.98	3.66
50	Louisville	2.76	2.55	3.12	3.08	2.64	2.76	3.63
40	Oklahoma City	2.98	2.98	2.98	3.02	3.12	2.69	3.59
39	Orlando	2.35	2.92	3.04	3.60	2.85	2.87	3.54
56	Cape Coral/Fort Myers/Naples	2.42	2.68	2.23	3.03	2.80	2.87	3.45
28	Washington, DC—Northern VA	2.62	3.49	3.19	3.29	2.98	3.04	3.45
55	Jacksonville	2.34	2.21	3.05	2.71	2.60	2.98	3.31
51	Washington, DC—MD suburbs	2.46	2.94	2.46	3.30	2.39	2.87	3.29
63	Richmond	2.44	2.37	2.75	2.81	2.25	2.62	3.27
59	Birmingham	2.30	2.60	2.98	2.62	2.34	2.85	3.20
72	Virginia Beach/Norfolk	2.54	2.66	2.35	2.94	2.34	1.89	3.17
34	Columbia	3.28	3.16	3.15	2.51	2.98	2.98	3.04
69	Memphis	2.13	2.13	2.98	2.64	2.17	2.49	2.80
70	Deltona/Daytona	1.70	2.27	2.44	2.92	2.69	2.48	2.76
35	**South average**	**2.86**	**2.99**	**3.11**	**3.22**	**2.87**	**3.10**	**3.68**

Source: *Emerging Trends in Real Estate 2015* survey.

*Average score of local market participants' opinion on strength of local economy, investor demand, capital availability, development and redevelopment opportunities, public/private investments, and local development community.

The office sector scores well in a number of the regional markets included in the top 20, but survey respondents were less optimistic for the region as a whole. A number of office markets in the region received comparatively low scores, but the survey respondents are a little more positive about office opportunities in San Antonio, Columbia, and Charleston.

Exhibit 3-16 **Local Market Perspective: Development/ Redevelopment Opportunities**

Weak	Declining	Average	Improving	Strong

City	Rating	City	Rating
Houston	4.62	Phoenix	3.57
Dallas/Fort Worth	4.24	Salt Lake City	3.55
San Jose	4.20	Washington, DC—District	3.54
Seattle	4.19	Portland, OR	3.54
New Orleans	4.17	Tampa/St. Petersburg	3.52
New York—Brooklyn	4.15	Inland Empire	3.51
Denver	4.14	Philadelphia	3.51
San Francisco	4.09	St. Louis	3.50
Nashville	4.06	Orlando	3.48
Minneapolis/St. Paul	4.05	Cincinnati	3.47
Los Angeles	4.00	Northern New Jersey	3.43
Miami	4.00	Jacksonville	3.43
Pittsburgh	4.00	Cape Coral/Fort Myers/Naples	3.43
Oklahoma City	4.00	Tacoma	3.40
Louisville	4.00	Deltona/Daytona	3.33
Raleigh/Durham	3.98	Cleveland	3.30
Austin	3.94	Honolulu	3.25
Indianapolis	3.90	Sacramento	3.18
San Diego	3.85	Las Vegas	3.17
Charlotte	3.84	Milwaukee	3.17
Oakland/East Bay	3.84	Spokane	3.17
Boston	3.81	Birmingham	3.17
Charleston	3.81	Washington, DC—Northern VA	3.15
Columbus	3.80	Buffalo	3.14
Kansas City, MO	3.78	Richmond	3.10
Madison	3.75	Virginia Beach/Norfolk	3.09
New York—Manhattan	3.75	Washington, DC—MD suburbs	3.07
Chicago	3.74	Baltimore	3.03
Atlanta	3.72	Des Moines	3.00
Orange County	3.71	Westchester/Fairfield, NY/CT	3.00
Boise	3.70	Columbia	3.00
Omaha	3.67	Hartford	3.00
New York—other boroughs	3.65	Memphis	2.92
San Antonio	3.65	Portland, ME	2.88
Palm Beach	3.64	Albuquerque	2.73
Greenville	3.63	Tucson	2.33
Fort Lauderdale	3.63	Providence	1.75
Detroit	3.62		

Source: *Emerging Trends in Real Estate 2015* survey.

Property Type Outlook

"The collaborative aspect of open space is overdone.

I don't think people need to talk to their coworkers all day long."

In the course of a 162-game season, major league baseball teams know that even the best clubs are going to wind up losing five dozen games or more. The late baseball commissioner A. Bartlett Giamatti said of the sport, "Baseball is designed to break your heart." Indeed, is there any other pastime where failure is so expected that errors are posted in every day's box score? Where an offensive player is counted as superior if he makes out merely seven times out every ten attempts? Where a pitcher is credited with a "quality start" if he allows just three runs and completes six out of the game's nine innings?

Because of this expectation of disappointment, positive streaks stand out. Statisticians, in their cold, analytical way, say that streaks are mathematically normal. But every batter in an inning's rally and every pitcher handed the ball the day after a win has one phrase in mind: "Keep the line moving." Winning is thought to be contagious, and it is one syndrome that everyone wants to experience.

Real estate's current winning streak started with the multifamily sector, and we have been watching the other property types queue up in their turn. In 2014, *Emerging Trends* sounded the theme "Gaining Momentum." This year, we see the industry's momentum broadening to encompass many more individual markets, and most property types. Momentum—mass times velocity, in the classical formula of physics—can be viewed by measures of size and measures of speed. Let's look at the trends emergent in each property type and get a sense of real estate as it accelerates into 2015.

Industrial

One of the basic principles of market analysis is that of equilibrium. Like so many things in life, the business of real estate is a balancing act. The principle of equilibrium says that market

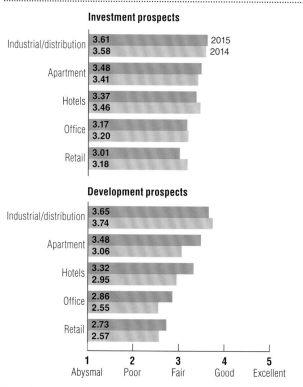

Exhibit 4-1 **Prospects for Major Commercial Property Types, 2015 vs. 2014**

Source: *Emerging Trends in Real Estate* surveys.

Note: Based on U.S. respondents only.

operations will lead toward the price point where supply and demand match up. This fundamental rule supports everything from the theory of cycles to the concept of "reversion to the mean." It lurks in the background of every discussion of excess

Exhibit 4-2 Prospects for Commercial/Multifamily Subsectors in 2015

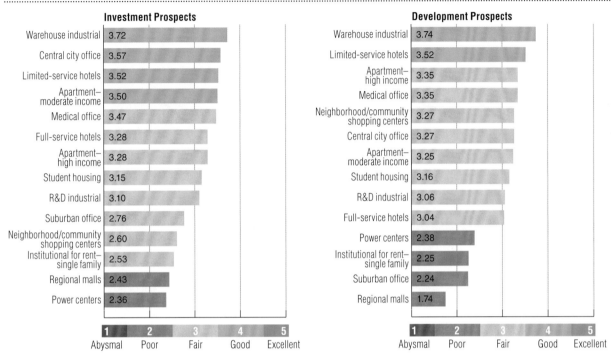

Investment Prospects

Warehouse industrial	3.72
Central city office	3.57
Limited-service hotels	3.52
Apartment—moderate income	3.50
Medical office	3.47
Full-service hotels	3.28
Apartment—high income	3.28
Student housing	3.15
R&D industrial	3.10
Suburban office	2.76
Neighborhood/community shopping centers	2.60
Institutional for rent—single family	2.53
Regional malls	2.43
Power centers	2.36

Development Prospects

Warehouse industrial	3.74
Limited-service hotels	3.52
Apartment—high income	3.35
Medical office	3.35
Neighborhood/community shopping centers	3.27
Central city office	3.27
Apartment—moderate income	3.25
Student housing	3.16
R&D industrial	3.06
Full-service hotels	3.04
Power centers	2.38
Institutional for rent—single family	2.25
Suburban office	2.24
Regional malls	1.74

1	2	3	4	5
Abysmal	Poor	Fair	Good	Excellent

Source: *Emerging Trends in Real Estate 2015* survey.

Note: Based on U.S. respondents only.

Exhibit 4-3 Prospects for Niche and Multiuse Property Types, 2015

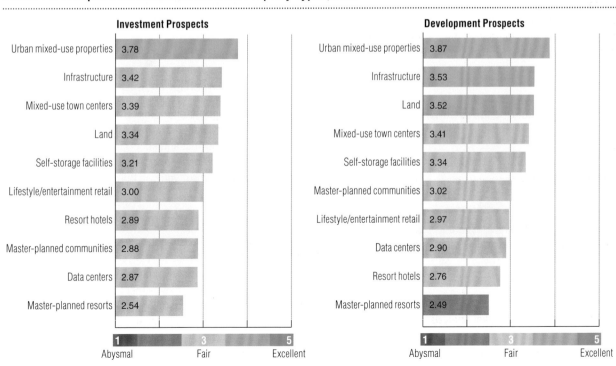

Investment Prospects

Urban mixed-use properties	3.78
Infrastructure	3.42
Mixed-use town centers	3.39
Land	3.34
Self-storage facilities	3.21
Lifestyle/entertainment retail	3.00
Resort hotels	2.89
Master-planned communities	2.88
Data centers	2.87
Master-planned resorts	2.54

Development Prospects

Urban mixed-use properties	3.87
Infrastructure	3.53
Land	3.52
Mixed-use town centers	3.41
Self-storage facilities	3.34
Master-planned communities	3.02
Lifestyle/entertainment retail	2.97
Data centers	2.90
Resort hotels	2.76
Master-planned resorts	2.49

1	3	5
Abysmal	Fair	Excellent

Source: *Emerging Trends in Real Estate 2015* survey.

Note: Based on U.S. respondents only.

Exhibit 4-4 Moody's/RCA Commercial Property Price Index, by Sector

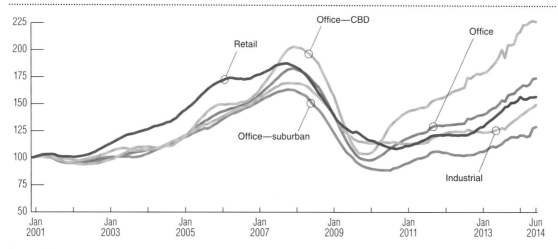

Sources: Moody's and Real Capital Analytics.
Note: Updated August 2014; data through June 2014.

or deficiency. It is also—critically so—what keeps real estate dynamic, the source of risk as well as opportunity.

So far, that's Econ 101. What makes real estate so especially interesting, for good or ill, is that it is "asynchronous." It takes time for supply to adjust to demand, so the market can stay out of balance for considerable periods of time. Sometimes real estate strays far from equilibrium, leaving real estate practitioners to cope with extreme dislocations for quite some time. That is where real money can be made or lost.

For the industrial property type, that balancing act could be getting very tricky very soon. As the graph illustrating historical and projected supply/demand fundamentals shows, since 2010 this

Exhibit 4-5 U.S. Industrial: Change in Supply and Demand

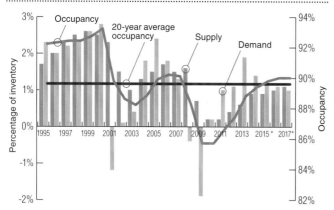

Source: CBRE Econometric Advisors.
*Forecasts.

vast (more than 12 billion square feet of space) sector has enjoyed a rising demand trend and supply additions that have not kept pace. Come 2015, however, industrials are entering a period when projected construction is accelerating, but demand is anticipated to decelerate. What's the right price to pay under those circumstances? What do you do when two most relevant trends diverge?

Last year, our interviewees and survey respondents really liked industrials. For many, that has not changed. A public sector pension fund executive still has this sector as a top choice, seeing 2015 as a period of active buying, developing, and rehabbing of space. A New England–based investment manager who focuses solely on office and industrial properties is bullish on the warehousing sector this year, projecting that it "could be the most sought-after property type in commercial real estate, doing very well and continuing to do so even with some new supply." Midwest and secondary markets such as Nashville, St. Louis, Charlotte, and Louisville provide cap-rate premiums in his view, while "you can build industrial in these markets and get good returns."

Views like these account for the industrial sector standing atop the sector rankings for investment, with a robust score of 3.61 in this year's *Emerging Trends* survey (exhibit 4-1). Moreover, in the more granular subsector evaluation, warehouses posted an even higher rating of 3.72 for investment and 3.74 for development (exhibit 4-2). In each case, these results were well ahead of the second-place choices.

Exhibit 4-6 **U.S. Industrial Property Total Returns**

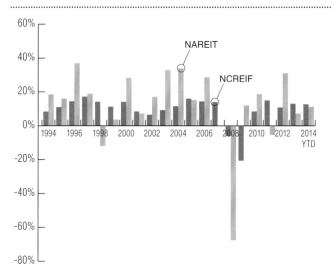

Sources: NCREIF Fund Index Open-End Diversified Core (ODCE) NAREIT Equity REIT Index.
*Returns as of June 30, 2014.

A renowned valuation/consultant figure reinforces this viewpoint. "Logistic space demand [is] growing steadily. Warehouse cap rates are 'dropping like a rock.' Investors like the stable cash flow, and retailers need the goods." Given international trade volumes, he likes industrial properties near ports. Many others like the evolving relationship between industrial and retail. "Industrial is cannibalizing retail sales as internet commerce grows. How does the same-day-delivery effort impact megasized distribution facilities? Will we see the return of smaller break-bulk facilities versus the major distributor air-hub strategy? And what about 'reverse logistics' as vendors promise consumers 'free return' of unwanted purchases?" Simplistic Econ 101 supply/demand graphs are not going to provide useful answers to such complex questions.

Some trends highlighted in *Emerging Trends 2014* remain solidly in place. The return of manufacturing activity to the United States with the associated evolution of our economic relationship with China prompted affirmation among this year's interviewees. This trend is positive for several regions. A prominent investment strategist sees a revival in the Midwest, and a top broker has a similar observation about the Carolinas and Tennessee stimulating a whole roster of suppliers. Industrial real estate markets are in robust shape. A real estate investment trust (REIT) executive sees the return of manufacturing helping not just the United States but also Mexico, which was undercut by lower costs available in the Asian labor markets. Though some still consider "onshoring" to be only anecdotal at this point, others think some very basic factors point to its sustainability as a trend:

Exhibit 4-7 **Industrial/Distribution Investment Prospect Trends**

Source: *Emerging Trends in Real Estate* surveys.

U.S. warehouse industrial

2015	Prospects	Rating	Ranking
Investment prospects	3.72	Good	1
Development prospects	3.74	Good	1

Buy 57.6%	Hold 29.9%	Sell 12.5%

Expected capitalization rate, December 2015   6.2%

U.S. R&D industrial

2015	Prospects	Rating	Ranking
Investment prospects	3.10	Fair	9
Development prospects	3.06	Fair	9

Buy 26.0%	Hold 48.0%	Sell 26.0%

Expected capitalization rate, December 2015   7.0%

Source: *Emerging Trends in Real Estate 2015* survey.
Note: Based on U.S. respondents only.

- The decline of labor as a percentage of product cost;

- Rising shipping expenses;

- Lower energy costs in the United States bolstering our advantage; and

- Intellectual property security—or lack thereof—in the Asian nations.

Those rising shipping expenses ripple through the distribution sector, where logistics firms seek "better, faster, cheaper" paths from producer to consumer. This has tempered the optimism about the overwhelmingly positive effects of the deeper and wider Panama Canal—and the Panamax container vessels plying it. East Coast ports now face some sobering numbers. The logistics chain has many, many interlocking parts—among them, the multibillion-dollar expansion and modernization of the canal cost big. Shippers will have to face higher tolls, with the levy for the largest ships roughly tripling from a reported $375,000 to $1 million. Not all the upland improvements on the East Coast will be ready in 2015 and 2016, reducing efficiency and adding to cost. It's going to take some ports a while to realize the anticipated shipping benefits. Taking into account the existing infrastructure on the West Coast, one observer noted, "You can see why Warren Buffet bought a railroad."

The industrial sector is far from boring. It is still rated a solid "buy" among *Emerging Trends* survey respondents, and has been sustaining double-digit returns to investors in both the National Council of Real Estate Investment Fiduciaries (NCREIF) and National Association of Real Estate Investment Trusts (NAREIT) indexes. On balance it all looks very good—for now.

Hotels

The prospects for liquidity in the hospitality sector shape up as excellent for 2015. Our survey respondents would be quite happy to hold hotel assets, and there is good balance on the buy/sell recommendations for full-service hotels. Limited-service hotels have upside in pricing, if the spread of 31.6 percent of "buy" advocates over 23.9 percent "sell" proponents is a proxy for bid/ask pressure. Remarkably, and in distinct comparison with most other property types, the survey shows no expectation of any alteration in cap rates for hotels—not even a basis point. How often does that happen? The expected cap rates for December 2015 are anticipated to stand at 7.1 percent for limited-service hotels and 6.6 percent for full-service lodging facilities.

Hotels have been in high favor, and have seen exceptional demand. Transaction volume tracked by Real Capital Analytics was up 24.1 percent through July 2014, compared with the same year-to-date figure for 2013. A few major transactions pushed the full-service sector up 28.8 percent while the limited-service segment was up 14.3 percent in total dollar volume. In all, $18.4 billion in hotel deals was concluded over the first seven months of 2014. This is a volatile sector, though, and closely correlated with gross domestic product (GDP). While the economic consensus is favorable for the next couple of years, this is a difficult sector to time—especially in an era when geopolitical events can stifle travel with just a few headlines.

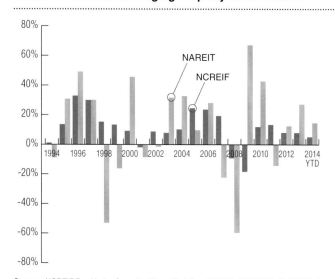

Exhibit 4-8 **U.S. Hotel/Lodging Property Total Returns**

Sources: NCREIF Fund Index Open-End Diversified Core (ODCE); NAREIT Equity REIT Index.
*Returns as of June 30, 2014.

An executive of a private REIT with exposure to the sector says, "From a lodging perspective, I see a 2 percent new supply in hotel space, which keeps us focused. There is no surprise that hotel numbers are growing in the cities, but it is concerning to see them ramping up in the suburbs right now." Nevertheless, he says, "Hotels will surprise on the upside at the end of 2014, and the same solid growth will continue into 2015."

Boutique hotels are sprouting up like wildflowers. For decades, the integrated reservation systems of the national chains made a "flag" a necessity for success in the hotel business. The internet changed that, as individuals became their own travel agents and could comparison-shop online. The standardization of the chains is a comforting factor for those who seek a "known commodity" in lodging (not to mention points in the affinity programs). But increasingly sophisticated travelers are seeking a more customized experience, a hotel that is "different" in layout, amenities, and theme.

The rise of online personal rentals aims right at the customer base seeking a nonstandard experience, with the significant twist of do-it-yourself (DIY) style travel. Low cost, obviously, lies at the heart of the market penetration question—and the potentially vast expansion of supply is an as-yet-unquantified threat to pricing in conventional facilities. One offsetting positive impact could be that lodging-sharing customers at the most inexpensive levels could be a net expansion of overall hospitality demand—travelers who were not likely to go on the road except for the "cheap and hip" crowdsourced option. The personal

Exhibit 4-9 Hotel Investment Prospect Trends

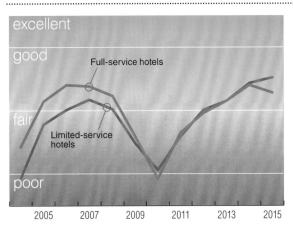

Source: *Emerging Trends in Real Estate* surveys.

U.S. limited-service hotels

2015	Prospects	Rating	Ranking
Investment prospects	3.52	Good	3
Development prospects	3.52	Good	2

Buy 31.6%	Hold 44.4%	Sell 23.9%

Expected capitalization rate, December 2015	7.1%

U.S. full-service hotels

2015	Prospects	Rating	Ranking
Investment prospects	3.28	Fair	6
Development prospects	3.04	Fair	10

Buy 30.3%	Hold 38.7%	Sell 31.1%

Expected capitalization rate, December 2015	6.6%

Source: *Emerging Trends in Real Estate 2015* survey.

Note: Based on U.S. respondents only.

rental industry estimates that 11 million people worldwide use its network. There's a lot of "buzz" associated with this short-term rental market in its exciting startup phase. But most products have a shake-out period when glitch meets buzz. That shakeout hasn't happened yet. Keep an eye on this niche product, but don't let it distract you from the economic basics that are the foundation of the traditional hospitality industry.

One developer/operator in the hotel field says, "At this point, it is cheaper to build than to buy." But costs are rising, especially in markets with strong economies based on energy or technology. Sites are expensive, permitting is slow, and skilled labor is in short supply. This Texas-based developer was particularly

sensitive to the deleterious consequences of cutting down on immigration, seeing this as constricting the flow of blue-collar workers—not just unskilled laborers, but also those with skills in plumbing, electrical work, and vertical construction.

That developer cited ample financing capacity for new projects, and enviable returns. Leveraged purchases of existing product can return internal rates of return (IRRs) in the upper teens, and new construction in the 20 percent–plus range. Loan-to-cost at 60 to 65 percent means substantial equity in the deal, and that is not bothersome to him. The money is there, and lower leverage means lower risk—always important in a cyclical business.

This year's *Emerging Trends* survey shows hotels rated strongly in participants' 2015 prospects for investment and development, especially in the limited-service category. For hotels, apparently, the welcome mat is out.

Apartments

Multifamily was unquestionably real estate's trendsetter in the first years of recovery. Now that apartments have reached a more mature phase of their cycle, we get to a more interesting period. More interesting, in the first place, because the investment/development questions become more complex and nuanced. And more interesting because it is probable that issues and strategies that will be tested in 2015 in the multifamily sector will help shape the template for 2016–2018 in other property types. Keep your eye on apartments this year.

If you go by just the numbers, the opinions of the *Emerging Trends* survey respondents seem sharply divided. For high-end

Exhibit 4-10 U.S. Multifamily: Change in Supply and Demand

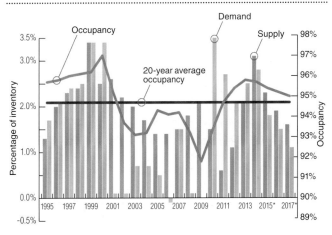

Source: REIS Inc.

*Forecasts.

Exhibit 4-11 U.S. Apartment Property Total Returns

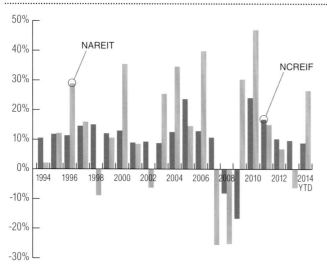

Sources: NCREIF Fund Index Open-End Diversified Core (ODCE); NAREIT Equity REIT Index.
*Returns as of June 30, 2014.

Exhibit 4-12 Apartment Investment Prospect Trends

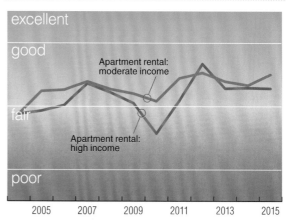

Source: *Emerging Trends in Real Estate* surveys.

U.S. high-income apartments

2015	Prospects	Rating	Ranking
Investment prospects	3.28	Fair	7
Development prospects	3.35	Fair	3

Buy 21.4%	Hold 30.4%	Sell 48.2%

Expected capitalization rate, December 2015	5.2%

U.S. moderate-income apartments

2015	Prospects	Rating	Ranking
Investment prospects	3.50	Good	4
Development prospects	3.25	Fair	7

Buy 35.2%	Hold 37.1%	Sell 27.7%

Expected capitalization rate, December 2015	6.0%

Source: *Emerging Trends in Real Estate 2015* survey.
Note: Based on U.S. respondents only.

multifamily, nearly half of the respondents (48 percent) felt it would be smart to divest in 2015, while 30 percent consider it worthwhile to hold for a longer period. Only 21 percent suggest this is a good time to buy. At the more moderate income level, that relationship was reversed. Only 28 percent recommend selling while holding and acquisition are more attractive, with 37 percent and 35 percent recommending these strategies, respectively, in the year ahead.

What gives? The survey subtly distinguishes between the moderate- and upper-income tiers' investment and development prospects. For investment, more moderately priced apartments have the edge, with a 3.50 rating versus the higher-income properties at 3.28. Despite this, the upper-income units have such an attractive price-to-cost spread that they have the edge in development prospects, 3.35 to 3.25.

Survey respondents expect upward cap-rate adjustment, though most of the shift will not happen in 2015 but in the 2016–2018 period. The sense of urgency to sell just isn't at hand right now. Although 48 percent think it's a good time to sell luxury, the coming year is not anticipated to see major change. Time to book profits remains. Impacts are forecast to be "at the margin." The luxury end has had cap rates driven down the most, and should expect greater cap-rate expansion—90 basis points— by 2018, while more middle-income properties face a rise of 70 basis points. The investment pricing differential, in other words, is expected to narrow as we go into the future. That's a trend to watch.

What might account for this? Developers' preferences for upper-end apartments notwithstanding, the depth of demand for luxury rental units goes only so far. Wealthy households prefer to own their homes—and most already do. The bulk of pent-up and emerging demand comes from the battered middle-income and lower-middle-income sector, predominantly renters. As the forecasted gains in employment take hold, millennial sharers, "boomerang children," domestic migrants, and international immigrants represent the bulk of new residential renter demand. Developers may actually be able to "make up in volume what they can't achieve in price."

The overarching context is that next year and beyond, the demand fundamentals for moderate apartments continue to look very good. Many interviewees expect the millennials to move into homeownership in some significant numbers, but that won't happen until 2020 or later.

One economic forecaster sees terrific opportunities to buy value-add multifamily and suggests as a "best bet" purchasing "B" buildings in "A" markets. The thinking is that such properties can be repositioned and that the overheated luxury market exerts upward pressure on even more modest rentals. Should the acceleration in the job market begin to push incomes up for the middle class—a hope or a reasonable guess, but not a certainty—there could be a nice bump in rents for those Class B apartment buildings.

Yes, supply is still on the rise. But that, too, is tiered, and a disproportionate share of new construction is at the high end. This makes sense when urban high-rise property in the gateway markets is priced at 20 to 30 percent more than the cost to construct. Of course, this spurs the developers on! Interestingly, though, the urban housing surge is now extending into the Nashvilles, Greenvilles, and Raleighs—cities where even until recently the central business district (CBD) emptied out in the evening as commuters returned to the suburbs in their cars. Now, while the cities themselves are still labeled "car dependent" by Walkscore.com, their downtowns have good to excellent walkability scores—and builders have caught on. One hallmark of these Southeast markets is their cost-competitiveness in comparison with the large coastal cities. Locally low cost of living, in turn, argues for moderate-rent apartments as the better investment opportunity.

Some earlier favorites are already victims of their own success. A local investment manager looks at Boston's lively apartment development scene and says, "Whoa! Too much!" And a veteran institutional investor looks at Washington, D.C., multifamily and sees one of the nation's biggest real estate risks for 2015. Sure enough, the *Emerging Trends* survey has Boston down in 20th place for multifamily investment prospects and 21st for development, and D.C. ranks 30th in investment prospects and 32nd for development. Several interviewees singled out Boston and Washington as multifamily markets that have "gotten ahead of themselves."

Interestingly, though, survey respondents still felt that both Boston and Washington represented "buy" opportunities, by 49 percent and 41 percent of the respondents, respectively—which must mean they are looking beyond 2015 to longer-term market strength. Otherwise, it is many of the "usual suspects" that are in the top 20 rankings, as well as many newcomers such as Nashville, Austin, San Jose, Orange County, Portland, and

Brooklyn (see Markets to Watch). Brooklyn, New York, ranked number one, has long been in the shadows of Manhattan's skyscrapers. It has become the "hip" borough in recent years as the young "creative class" element has been priced out of many Manhattan neighborhoods.

As a screening device, one investor looks for markets with science, technology, engineering, and math (STEM) strength—which usually means a big research university drawing young tech and engineering talent in need of apartments, with salaries that are attractive to the owners of rental complexes. The real strength in multifamily, though, is that it is not dependent upon just one demand segment. As local economies grow and the number of jobs rises, rental housing is required. This is not rocket science.

Unless you are a contrarian, though, don't expect a rapid upward turnaround for suburban garden apartments. Once a classic vehicle for developers and investors riding the wave out of the center city, these are now out of favor with millennial renters and portfolio managers alike. Still, transaction data show that there's a steady parade of buyers for garden apartment product, which has about a 150-basis-point-higher cap rate than mid- and high-rise multifamily. As potent as the urbanization trend is, there is still a huge base of suburban units out there—and they are a lot cheaper.

Retail

Investment and development strength in the retail sector ranks the lowest of all the major property types in the 2015 *Emerging Trends* survey. Just as the slow recovery in jobs has hindered

Exhibit 4-13 U.S. Retail: Change in Supply and Demand

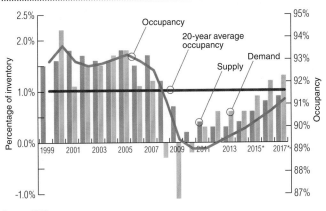

Source: REIS.

*Forecasts.

Exhibit 4-14 U.S. Retail Property Total Returns

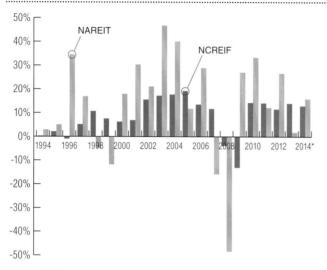

Sources: NCREIF Fund Index Open-End Diversified Core (ODCE); NAREIT Equity REIT Index.
*Returns as of June 30, 2014.

Exhibit 4-15 Retail Investment Prospect Trends

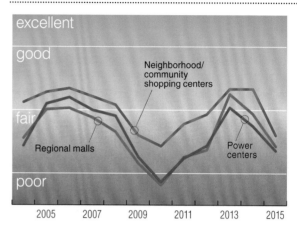

Source: *Emerging Trends in Real Estate* surveys.

U.S. neighborhood/community centers

2015	Prospects	Rating	Ranking
Investment prospects	2.60	Fair	11
Development prospects	3.27	Fair	5

Buy 47.3%	Hold 35.4%	Sell 17.3%

Expected capitalization rate, December 2015   6.6%

U.S. power centers

2015	Prospects	Rating	Ranking
Investment prospects	2.36	Poor	14
Development prospects	2.38	Poor	11

Buy 14.6%	Hold 39.5%	Sell 45.9%

Expected capitalization rate, December 2015   6.7%

U.S. regional malls

2015	Prospects	Rating	Ranking
Investment prospects	2.43	Poor	13
Development prospects	1.74	Poor	14

Buy 9.1%	Hold 38.3%	Sell 52.6%

Expected capitalization rate, December 2015   6.5%

Source: *Emerging Trends in Real Estate 2015* survey.
Note: Based on U.S. respondents only.

many other economic growth indicators, so too has the jobs recovery made real estate professionals wary of calling a bounce back in retail. Optimism has seemed premature—or even unrealistic. It is time to question that. The trend for retail for the second half of this decade should be a story of expectations exceeded—expectations that continue to be set too low by those wounded in the last battle.

Many fall into that camp, including a substantial cadre of *Emerging Trends* interviewees. Even in the surging Southeast markets, things still seem very slow to some top brokers. You can hear the caution in one such voice: "The suburban retail overhang has mostly been absorbed, but prices are low. There is some opportunity in 'shadow-anchored' space, such as pads close to big boxes. Successful deals are purely driven by national anchors. But, on balance, it is still slow." An investment manager observes, "Retail is a worrisome sector. Consumer preferences are so volatile that obsolescence comes ever more quickly." A top executive recruiter with an overview of the industry is concerned about the context of our economic structure: "In the U.S., there is this increasing story of haves and have-nots. Office and retail are both impacted by this divide." An institutional investor reveals that his portfolio allocation to retail has dropped to just 5 percent—one dollar out of every 20 available for acquisition. The chief investment officer of a public pension fund concurs, "Retail is our least favored property sector."

Such trepidations may be entirely understandable. But they may also be out of step with changes in fundamentals and with sentiment shifts that are likely to alter the direction of retail property trends.

Like every other property type, retail has its cyclical ups and downs. But one REIT CEO urges keeping an eye on the big picture. "America averages an increase of 3 million–plus in population annually. We'll be up by 100 million come 2050. What does this mean for retail real estate? More groceries, more drugstores, more outlets for goods of all kinds." An investment manager thinks that as job growth becomes more self-sustaining in 2015, retail will benefit from pent-up demand, saying, "There's a lot of 'alpha' in shopping centers." An East Coast pension fund executive is convinced that retail is "in recovery," and is placing money alongside retail specialists in properties it considers undercapitalized but poised for a turnaround.

An officer with an international investment fund sees the retail sector in transition. "The retail property sector may be poised to outperform in 2015. Its business model is adjusting to multichannel retailing. Obsolete retail is transitioning to other uses. The consumer looks poised to be in better shape in 2015." Then he makes a most intriguing comment—one that suggests that the template of multifamily and office investment distribution will appear in the retail sector soon. "Interest will remain in gateway markets, but the increase in capital will likely begin to move to more secondary markets." As the ball players say, "Keep the line moving."

As the shift in trend takes hold, attention to detail is critical.

Urban/high street. Anyone who hasn't focused on how radically downtown retailing has changed has missed one of the great stories of the early 21st century. Remember when everyone lamented the "hollowing out" of the downtowns, and the nostalgia for the iconic department stores that anchored Main Street? Main Street has come back big time. If the millennial wave has the influence that is expected over the next ten to 15 years, the high street revival trend is just gathering force. This trend is not to be missed, especially as those smaller cities willing to promote downtown residential density join the parade. A Mid-Atlantic investment manager calls urban retailing one of the winners, a top prospect for 2015. A colleague calls this sector one where e-commerce is a boost rather than a drain. Some see the nation's top retail streets as being as much display or advertising as they are distribution points. Others aren't so sure, pointing to the large number of international tourists carrying goods home. And the notion that "high street" is all about luxury goods needs to be revisited, says a prominent retail broker. "Just walk down Fifth Avenue or North Michigan Avenue and actually

take a look at the tenants—then tell me that the middle market isn't being served!"

Neighborhood/community centers. In contrast to regional malls and power centers, neighborhood and community centers are rated a "buy" by a 47.3 percent plurality of this year's *Emerging Trends* survey respondents. And they feel that such centers have relatively less exposure to cap-rate expansion than other retail property, and indeed most other commercial property types. That's a very favorable outlook for the future. Although these smaller shopping centers rate only 2.60 as an investment prospect according to our survey respondents, development prospects are a stronger 3.27—the same as CBD office. That reflects survey respondents' confidence in future growth in spending power.

Flexibility in use is seen as a key to the future. Brick-and-mortar retailing is increasingly about service, convenience, "experience," tangibility, and linked demand. So medical services combine with drugstores, healthy-product retailers, and even athletic-oriented stores in a new tenant array. A public pension fund is seeking undercapitalized retail assets, provided they believe in the local market. "We like grocery-anchored, pharmacy-anchored [preferably both] centers," says that institutional investor, "and we also like to see the tenants invest their own money to upgrade their facilities." So add "alignment of interests" to the deal desiderata. One of the leading pension fund consultants smiles on such a strategy, but notes that such transactions "are very hard to come by."

What makes sense near a power discounter? Maybe DIY chains or a restaurant, thinks an industry executive. "Dollar stores" have been shadowing power discounters for some time, seeking to capture some of the spending of value-oriented buyers. A Midwest specialist in strip centers observes, "The big-box format is maturing. These category-killers were a huge shock, but surviving competitors have figured out how to coexist." And to no one's surprise, these power discounters are counterpunching with an aggressive program rolling out hundreds of smaller stores. They are making their presence felt in mixed-use developments and in downtown shopping districts.

In the face of urbanization trends, some investors are seeing the neighborhood/community center as a chance to get a "bite-sized piece of an outward-facing city"—an interesting characterization of the many U.S. metro areas still expanding on their perimeters, including Charlotte or northern Virginia. One of the great opportunities in real estate is its diversity of scale. Bigger is not always better. A wide range of investors and developers can find a market niche for themselves.

Malls. On a scale of 1 to 5 (where 5 is best), regional malls are rated just 2.43 for investment and 1.74 for development in 2015, with more than half (52.6 percent) of the survey respondents recommending "sell" and only 9.1 percent advising "buy." One Wall Street specialist sees this as painting with too broad a brush. "Don't buy generalizations pooh-poohing Class B malls. In places like Chattanooga and Minot [North Dakota], these may be consumers' only option and still a center of suburban activity." An asset manager echoes the sentiment: "In secondary and tertiary markets, stick to absolutely best retail properties. High-quality malls are always good; but now more of the busted retail properties are seeking to reposition." That's an acute perspective, and one shared by some top names. Malls are viewed as being in a binary state. Opportunity funds seem to be seeking turnarounds, and some notable firms have been aggressively accumulating mall assets. A Midwest broker speaks of "quality bifurcation," and at least one interviewee remarked that "bifurcation seems to be a permanent feature of the market."

E-commerce and multichannel distribution. The fear factor concerning the internet is subsiding noticeably. The adaptation of traditional retailers to e-commerce is now well advanced. To the surprise of many, there is the countervailing trend of e-merchants opening stores. The "pop-up store" phenomenon is turning out to be an interesting experimental approach for nascent brands to sample the "bricks" side of retailing as a complement to "clicks." The internet turns out to be a great venue for innovation, with a positive real estate outcome for winners who survive the online sorting-out process.

"E-commerce has hit certain parts of retail but not across the board; people still like to congregate and buy and touch," said a pension plan sponsor. Who should be more prone to internet shopping than the urban hipster? However, one retail veteran pointed out, "Technology [e-commerce] is not impacting what I develop. Right now, urban retailers' priority is to break into new locations." That's real places, not virtual places. The trendiest spots still blossom with boutiques, coffee shops, ethnic restaurants, and other experiential retail that just cannot be duplicated in cyberspace. You can't eat the internet.

The whole point of merchandise distribution is to get to customers with comprehensive coverage, speed, and service. If e-commerce now represents about 9.5 percent of consumer sales, merchants are well aware that stores account for more than 90 percent. That's opportunity. Still, some savvy interviewees look at the growth of e-commerce as potentially doubling in market share, and think that internet retailing should be rated a "best bet." Let the debate continue!

Exhibit 4-16 U.S. Office: Change in Supply and Demand

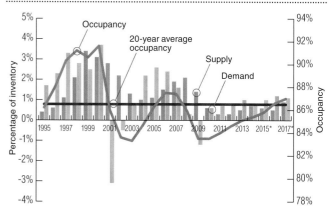

Source: CBRE Econometric Advisors.
*Forecasts.

Offices

Offices—CBD offices in particular, and CBD offices in the leading 24-hour cities especially—followed apartments in the lineup of property types cycling upward after the financial crisis. This would be no surprise to *Emerging Trends* readers, interviewees, and survey respondents, since it was this publication that brought the concept of "24-hour real estate markets" to public attention 20 years ago. It is gratifying, however, to see that the academic literature is finally catching up to the industry's intuition and experience. Papers in such respected publications as the *Journal of Real Estate Portfolio Management* have been testing and validating the claim, published here in our 1995 edition, that 24-hour cities would provide superior investment performance. The live/work/play theme is not just hype; it is statistically significant.

In fact, that might very well be one of the more powerful trends for offices, and not just in the gateway cities. The resurgence in downtown living is bolstering secondary office markets around the country. It turns out that workers like the urban feel and lunchtime amenities better than employee cafeterias. Moreover, as transit-oriented developments become more common, more-complex urban centers with a variety of uses provide "externalities" that enhance "quality of work life" while buttressing office building values.

Austin, ranked tops for both office investment and development in this year's survey, has garnered national and international recognition as a live/work/play downtown. Houston, ranked number two, has effected an incredible downtown transformation and is one of America's most diverse and globally connected cities. One cross-border investor characterized Houston as "the

Exhibit 4-17 U.S. Office Property Total Returns

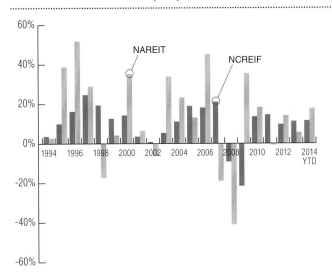

Sources: NCREIF Fund Index Open-End Diversified Core (ODCE); NAREIT Equity REIT Index.
*Returns as of June 30, 2014.

Exhibit 4-18 Office Investment Prospect Trends

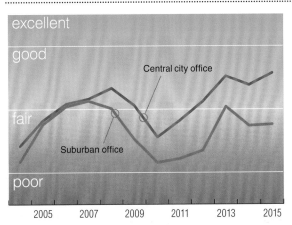

Source: *Emerging Trends in Real Estate* surveys.

U.S. central city office

2015	Prospects	Rating	Ranking
Investment prospects	3.57	Good	2
Development prospects	3.27	Fair	6

Buy 37.3%	Hold 34.0%	Sell 28.7%

Expected capitalization rate, December 2015	5.8%

U.S. suburban office

2015	Prospects	Rating	Ranking
Investment prospects	2.76	Fair	10
Development prospects	2.24	Poor	13

Buy 25.1%	Hold 32.7%	Sell 42.2%

Expected capitalization rate, December 2015	7.5%

Source: *Emerging Trends in Real Estate 2015* survey.
Note: Based on U.S. respondents only.

perfect storm for commercial real estate." Denver's LoDo neighborhood has helped concentrate that city's economic energy. A finance professional thinks that "Denver's discipline is better" than a number of other growth markets, and thus more capable of sustaining its upward trend.

Dallas, long the epitome of the edge-city configuration, is now seeking "to fully capitalize on the potential to be a 24-hour, 21st-century urban neighborhood" in its plan, Downtown Dallas 360. It is enlightening to see how similar the rankings for top cities are across property types, showing how a variety of land uses interact to create value. What a difference from the "separation of uses" zoning that influenced most cities in the last century. More and more, cities around the country are looking to stick with the mixed-use downtown winners—a reasonable basis for seeing this as a trend with decades to run.

Office activity has been strong in the first half of 2014, with Atlanta, Boston, Dallas, Denver, Houston, Los Angeles, and Manhattan all reporting good absorption levels. Rent growth is positive across the United States. With more than 77 million square feet under construction, the office inventory is expanding by 2 percent. A number of markets with especially high rent growth are also seeing rapid supply additions. Leading the list of office construction volume relative to existing inventory are Houston, San Jose, Austin, San Francisco, Seattle, Dallas/Fort Worth, and Nashville. The ratings of the *Emerging Trends* survey about office development markets match nicely with the observable data.

Office transaction volume was up 35 percent in the nation's downtowns and 25 percent in suburban markets through June 2014 compared to the same year-to-date figure for 2013, according to Real Capital Analytics (RCA). That investment preference is likely to continue, say our survey respondents. The "buy" recommendations for CBD and suburban office match the RCA volume data almost exactly, with 37 percent of the respondents saying it's a good time to buy CBD office and 25 percent recommending acquisition of suburban office. And while only 29 percent of survey respondents say that 2015 is a year to sell CBD office, 42 percent would sell office assets if they were in the suburbs. (Interestingly, the "hold" recommendations for downtown and suburbs are about the same at 34 percent.)

Exhibit 4-19 **Office Space under Construction as a Percentage of Total Inventory, 2Q 2014**

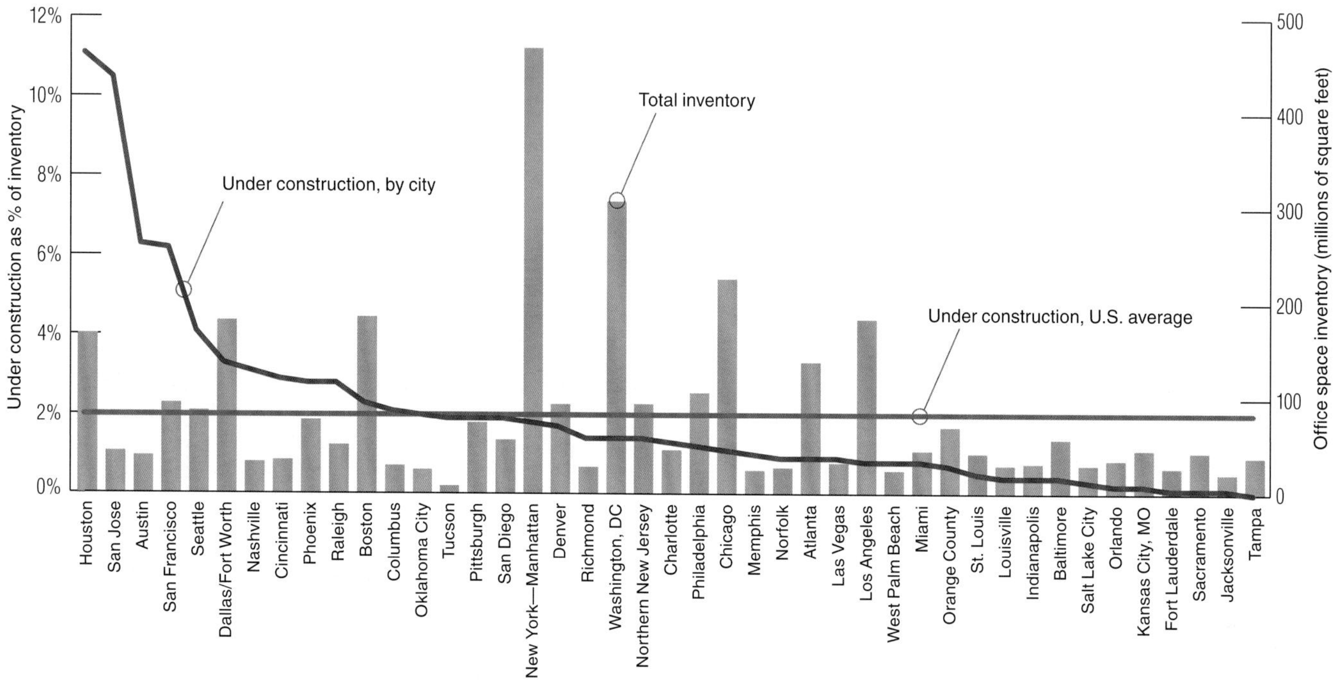

Source: CBRE Econometric Advisors.

That "sell the suburbs" call says a lot about the expectations for future trends.

Our interviewees season these numbers with their experience. A Midwest institutional investment officer explains, "Suburban office is not doing well for us. No one wants to buy it right now. The reemergence of suburban office is not likely soon, as the office sector is becoming more infill/urban, dense suburban, and less auto-dependent. "No one wants to pull into a big parking lot with no place to eat." The commodity-like character of many office parks is discounting their value, and impeding the ability of owners to drive rents upward. A Chicago-based interviewee describes the business parks around his city as "desolate." The millennial preference for downtowns contributes to the bleak outlook that some express for suburban office, and even recent trends toward office space compression have created problems—namely, parking allocations—for those suburban offices enjoying decent occupancy.

But we should have learned long ago to question assertions made with too broad a sweep. There is an articulate minority of the *Emerging Trends* interviewees who see suburban office "battling back," taking the position that "the death of suburban office has been greatly exaggerated," and seeing a contrarian opportunity for those investors willing to buck the majority

opinion. A Texas-based value-add investor is one of these: "Everybody seems to want a luxury car, but dealers sell an awful lot of sensible sedans." Perhaps a pension fund investor strikes a balance, in identifying dense clusters of offices linked to strong downtowns, a subset of the classic "edge cities" distinguished by being networked to healthy hubs, as the best opportunities. This investor names as examples such places as Tysons Corner, Virginia; Bellevue and Kirkland, Washington; and Mountain View, California.

Let us take one other observation from our interviewees that points to a trend that is bound to set off controversy. In a word, the drive toward space compression in office use is about at its end, and in the coming years the quality of the office environment will be used as a marketing tool to recruit talent. The millennial generation will not put up with the space cram-down much longer, especially as it gains seniority in the workforce. "We space" is going to have to accommodate "me space." Greater flexibility—and variety—in office space design will be superseding cost cutting as a prime imperative. "The collaborative aspect of open space is overdone," one interviewee noted. "I don't think people need to talk to their coworkers all day long."

Not all our interviewees agree with the perspective that space compression is nearing its limits. Feeling the recent trends still affecting future plans, one owner sees space sharing as being institutionalized in a profound way. "Companies such as WeWork are revolutionizing the way we think about office space." A global real estate asset manager ratifies this: "Technology plays a large role in office spaces since people are doing more with less space." A Northeast brokerage executive advises a nuanced view: "One size does not fit all when it comes to office space occupancy; firms are mixing/matching work-at-home, free-address locations in office, and management-directed floor planning." An institutional investor notes, "There is sure to be a different use of office space other than the old-fashioned kind of office space."

Nevertheless, our interviewees are signaling that it is time to re-examine what has become the conventional wisdom that cost control, higher worker densities, and worker bullpens are the wave of the future. That same institutional investor continued, "But the trend of no privacy and very high density is going to swing to the other direction." A peer with another institution concurs, "Office space compression has been a theme for more than 20 years. Be careful: people like to talk too readily about game-changers. We heard a lot about the paperless office."

A top broker in the Carolinas ran an interesting experiment with his staff. He asked his millennial staff members to design what his company's next office space should look like. All of them had private offices built into their plans, the "collaborative advantage" of open space notwithstanding. Inflection points—times when trends change—are notoriously difficult to pinpoint. But as startling as this claim may seem to some, a "back to the future" movement in space design could have an impact on offices as profound as the emergent 24-hour city movement of two decades ago. Forward-thinking real estate professionals should be alert for a tipping point in the space crunch, especially as the bidding for skilled workers intensifies over time.

And if the millennial generation's impact is still evolving, so too is the boomers'. While the Affordable Care Act's influence should not be ignored, the actuarial tables tell us that the need for medical care systematically increases with age. A REIT executive sees this as just a question of demographics: "People are getting older, and this favors medical offices and other forms of health care facilities."

The *Emerging Trends* survey respondents intuitively grasp the inexorable path of demand growth for medical offices, rating it at 3.5 in terms of investment prospects (right behind CBD offices) and at 3.3 for development, tied with downtown offices as a top choice. Moreover, medical office is seen as a "buy" for 2015 by 36.3 percent of respondents, and a "hold" by 40.6 percent,

with only 23.1 percent advising "sell." For one thing, medical office cap rates are expected to hold firm in 2015 at 6.6 percent, before experiencing the upward drift of cap rates that is an across-the-board expectation by 2018.

One private equity interviewee said this: "Medical office looks good on all metrics. We see a two-pronged trend where hospital campuses provide concentration for doctors, but diffusion [into communities, into malls] provides convenience for consumers. Health care is going to be 20 percent of GDP, so the real estate opportunity is great."

Housing

A minority opinion out there says, "The 'back to the city' trend is oversubscribed; not so many people care about walkability to a coffee shop; the majority of the U.S. is not on board with this. Don't discount housing affordability as a factor for families, and this disadvantages gateway cities." No doubt there's a kernel of truth there, and one size does not fit all. But keep in mind Damon Runyon's streetwise advice: "The battle is not always to the strong, nor the race to the swift—but that's the way to bet!" Housing is well on the way back, say the *Emerging Trends* survey respondents, and they rank urban/infill as the top opportunity for 2015.

Despite talk of lingering overindebtedness and the lack of savings on the part of potential homebuyers, the consensus reads this way: both for investment and for development, upper-income housing and moderate-income housing score equally well. Multifamily condominiums are just behind, and roughly in the same ballpark as affordable housing. An interviewee sees significant infill condo opportunities in 2015. A private equity investor thinks a serious look should be given to "condos where the markets haven't take off yet. Remember that millennials will become homeowners at some point, but where—city or suburb?" The answer is probably "both/and," not "either/or."

Condominium prices rose a modest 3.7 percent year over year during the second quarter of 2014, according to data from the National Association of Realtors. The inventory of condos for sale is very limited—just a 4.8 months' supply. Such a tight market, coupled with continued low interest rates (as expected), suggests a resumption of price escalation in the near future. Watch for that in 2015.

What is lagging? Exactly the sort of product that resort and retirement community developers were counting on as the baby boomers reached retirement age: golf course communities, second-home and leisure development, and the like. Who would have thought that the over-65 cohort would elect to

Exhibit 4-20 Prospects for Residential Property Types in 2015

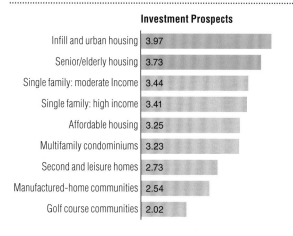

Investment Prospects

Property Type	Rating
Infill and urban housing	3.97
Senior/elderly housing	3.73
Single family: moderate Income	3.44
Single family: high income	3.41
Affordable housing	3.25
Multifamily condominiums	3.23
Second and leisure homes	2.73
Manufactured-home communities	2.54
Golf course communities	2.02

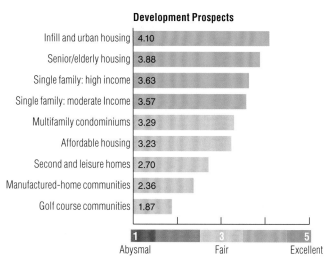

Development Prospects

Property Type	Rating
Infill and urban housing	4.10
Senior/elderly housing	3.88
Single family: high income	3.63
Single family: moderate Income	3.57
Multifamily condominiums	3.29
Affordable housing	3.23
Second and leisure homes	2.70
Manufactured-home communities	2.36
Golf course communities	1.87

1 Abysmal   3 Fair   5 Excellent

Source: *Emerging Trends in Real Estate 2015* survey.
Note: Based on U.S. respondents only.

return downtown from their suburban homes, instead of migrating to Florida and Arizona en masse? Further, both for financial reasons and because of an unwillingness to detach from work, boomers are staying in the workforce longer and in greater numbers than forecasted. That also has altered the housing picture for this cohort.

Developers are catching on. Outside the CBDs, urban village concepts are repositioning tired malls with ground-floor retail under small offices or residential units, complementing the mix with denser mid- to high-rise office, apartment, and hotel. Such mixed-use development approaches have been meeting with marked success.

The hangover of the housing bubble has not fully dissipated, and this will partially shape demand for the next several years. Even with jobs on the rise, doubling up in either parents' homes or with several roommates is an accepted norm, even if temporarily, for millennials. This version of a "new normal" is not forever, but it will linger because of the combination of high student loan indebtedness, meager wage and salary growth, and inadequate savings. Millennials who do desire the big backyard home will be deferring that dream into the 2020s if current trends are any indication. But valuing the quality of urban life does not necessarily mean wanting a tiny box in Manhattan forever. In that sense, the enthusiasm for "micro units" may be disappointing, prompting development of such units to be stalled in the thousands, rather than growing to millions nationally. A respectable middle course is bound to be found. One investor with a portfolio of single-family homes purchased in bulk for rental purposes believes that the millennial demand will be migrating to smaller cities, and can serve as that "middle course" transition product for those seeking greater affordability. He's ready for that trend.

Performance Snapshot of the Greenprint Office Portfolio: 2012–2013

Like for Like

Energy consumption

energy
-2.1%
2012: 5,501 million kWh
2013: 5,387 million kWh
Properties: 805

CO_2 emissions

carbon
-2.2%
2012: 2.2 million metric tonnes
2013: 2.1 million metric tonnes
Properties: 805

Cost

cost of energy
4.0%
2012: 337 million USD
2013: 350 million USD
Properties: 657

Electricity

electricity
-2.9%
2012: 4,462 million kWh
2013: 4,332 million kWh
Properties: 805

Water use

water
3.7%
2012: 7,004 million gallons
2013: 7,261 million gallons
Properties: 519

Density

occupancy
0.0%
2012: 94.3%
2013: 94.3%
Properties: 795

Emission Reduction Equivalents*

107,512
barrels of oil not consumed

9,733
cars taken off the road

4,218
homes not consuming energy

1,185,385
trees planted

22,524
metric tonnes of coal not burned

Source (for Performance Snapshot): ULI Greenprint Center. The mission of the ULI Greenprint Center for Building Performance is to lead the global real estate community toward value-enhancing carbon-reduction strategies.

*U.S. Environmental Protection Agency, Greenhouse Gas Equivalencies Calculator. www.epa.gov/cleanenergy/energy-resources/calculator.html.

Emerging Trends in Canada

"Everyone wants prime properties, but in the Canadian market the bidding on those can be quite competitive, so the market has gotten very creative in finding ways to enhance value."

No shocks and few surprises: As we look forward to 2015, the Canadian real estate market appears poised for another steady year. Canada's economy continues to deliver stable, modest growth, creating an ideal low-risk environment for real estate developers and investors.

Urbanization has become one of the key forces shaping Canada's real estate markets. Once viewed as an emerging trend, urbanization today is simply the "new normal." People are flooding into city cores to live close to both work and the lifestyle they crave. Now, companies and retailers are following them, and this is driving new office and commercial developments in the core. In turn, urbanization is blurring industry lines, as commercial and residential developers explore the opportunities that mixed-use properties bring.

Fueling all of this development is abundant investment capital and funding. Domestic and foreign investors alike are eager to pour their capital into new projects. Loan amounts are rising as banks become increasingly active—but no less discerning—lenders to high-quality commercial and residential projects. Pension funds and other institutional investors are looking to increase their real estate holdings. There are concerns, however, especially when eager but inexperienced lenders or investors team up with equally inexperienced developers to bring projects to market.

From a regional perspective, western Canada continues to be the country's economic engine. Alberta markets are strong, propelled by Calgary's office boom and significant development—from offices to condos to museums and a National Hockey League (NHL) arena—in Edmonton's core. Vancouver, on the cusp of an economic resurgence, has several office developments coming onto the market, while foreign investment continues to pour into its robust housing sector. Saskatoon is enjoying record housing sales and long-awaited growth in industrial space.

Exhibit 5-1 Real Estate Business Prospects for 2015

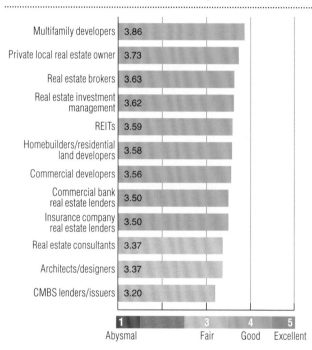

Multifamily developers	3.86
Private local real estate owner	3.73
Real estate brokers	3.63
Real estate investment management	3.62
REITs	3.59
Homebuilders/residential land developers	3.58
Commercial developers	3.56
Commercial bank real estate lenders	3.50
Insurance company real estate lenders	3.50
Real estate consultants	3.37
Architects/designers	3.37
CMBS lenders/issuers	3.20

1 Abysmal   3 Fair   4 Good   5 Excellent

Source: *Emerging Trends in Real Estate 2015* survey.
Note: Based on Canadian investors only.

In the east, Toronto's condo market remains strong and stable as people continue to flock downtown. And retailers are following, eager to deliver the services and amenities that core-dwellers demand. In Montreal, the office market will coast along while condo development slows as the market continues to absorb the new inventory—yet retail is expected to undergo significant development and change. Halifax's office market is looking bright, offsetting reduced confidence in the housing market.

Table 5-1 **2015 Forecast Economic Indicators**

	Real GDP growth (%)	Total employment growth (%)	Unemployment rate (%)	Personal income per capita growth (%)	Population growth (%)	Total housing starts	Retail sales growth (%)
Halifax	3.4%	2.2%	5.7%	3.7%	0.9%	2,017	4.9%
Vancouver	3.3%	2.6%	6.0%	3.5%	1.7%	18,040	4.9%
Calgary	3.1%	1.9%	4.7%	2.8%	2.1%	13,547	5.3%
Edmonton	3.0%	1.9%	4.8%	2.9%	1.9%	12,559	5.1%
Saskatoon	2.9%	0.7%	4.3%	1.1%	2.6%	3,210	4.5%
Toronto	2.9%	2.4%	7.2%	3.1%	1.9%	34,576	4.2%
Winnipeg	2.8%	1.9%	5.4%	3.1%	1.4%	4,266	3.5%
Montreal	2.5%	1.7%	7.6%	3.4%	0.9%	14,855	4.2%
Ottawa	1.9%	1.6%	5.9%	3.3%	0.8%	6,478	3.5%

Source: Conference Board of Canada.

Exhibit 5-2 **Emerging Trends Barometer 2015**

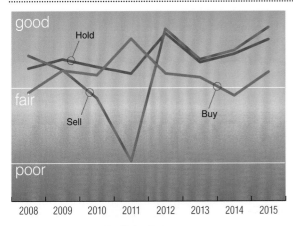

Source: *Emerging Trends in Real Estate 2015* survey.

Note: Based on Canadian investors only.

Looking ahead, what are the likely best bets in Canadian real estate? Western Canada will remain the place to be, buoyed by strong performance in Calgary and Edmonton. Commercial and office space on the edges of the urban core looks promising—as long as it's the right price. Speculative industrial appears strong in Alberta and the western part of Greater Toronto. Those focused on Toronto opportunities would do well to explore retail opportunities as well as multiresidential opportunities along transit corridors. And in a country with an aging population, seniors' housing—well managed and in good locations—offers attractive potential.

The Business Environment

Canada is enjoying stable economic growth, with a number of factors driving activity in the regions across the country. Future economic growth will benefit from ongoing immigration and the now-stronger U.S. economy. Despite these positives, concerns remain over the potential impact of fiscal constraints being implemented to deal with government deficits.

Economy

The Canadian economy remains stable overall, achieving modest growth and creating a low-risk business environment for developers and investors. The technology industry continues to contribute to growth in British Columbia's Greater Vancouver region, while oil and gas continue to be Alberta's economic engine. The financial sector and government spending are responsible for a significant portion of economic activity in both Ontario and Quebec; and in Atlantic Canada, shipbuilding and new oil and gas drilling are expected to provide a boost to the region's economy.

The broad manufacturing sector continues to shrink, as manufacturers move more production to lower-cost labor markets in the United States and elsewhere. This ongoing economic shift has had a profound impact on central Canada, particularly Ontario. Once the nation's economic engine, Ontario's economy now supports and benefits from the new growth powerhouses in western Canada.

Global economies also will likely have an impact in Canada. Canada as a whole and Ontario in particular are likely to get a boost from a stronger U.S. economy, which appears to be finally reaching a point of sustainable economic growth. On the other hand, there may be headwinds with Europe's continuing economic struggles and concerns around China's economy.

Table 5-2 Employment, Job Vacancy, and Average Weekly Earnings Growth, Year over Year

	Total employment growth	Job vacancy growth	Average weekly earnings growth
Canada	**0.5%**	**6.6%**	**2.4%**
Alberta	3.2%	4.7%	3.3%
Saskatchewan	2.1%	4.0%	2.7%
Ontario	0.6%	17.2%	1.7%
British Columbia	0.4%	17.2%	2.5%
Manitoba	-0.4%	4.0%	4.1%
New Brunswick	-0.5%	2.3%	2.8%
Quebec	-0.6%	-9.7%	1.6%
Prince Edward Island	-1.3%	33.3%	0.5%
Nova Scotia	-1.9%	15.2%	3.5%
Newfoundland/Labrador	-3.8%	8.3%	5.5%

Source: Statistics Canada, May 2014.

The energy sector will continue to play a large—and growing—role in the Canadian economy in the years to come. Asian markets, especially China, will become more important to Canada's energy sector as U.S. shale development makes the American market less reliant on Canada's energy production. However, the issue of how to transport Canadian oil and gas to both U.S. and non-U.S. markets still needs to be solved, and this could have a significant impact on the sector's fortunes. As well, uncertainties around Middle East stability will be a major factor in whether Canadian energy developments are economically feasible.

And as the hub of the country's economic growth has shifted to western Canada, so, too, have most of the employment opportunities. Interviewees noted that competition for scarce workers is already putting upward pressure on real estate construction costs, as builders find themselves competing with energy and natural resources firms for scarce skilled workers. Project timelines also will be negatively affected by the scarcity of labor.

"We're seeing the pressures in terms of skilled labor supply and demand," says an executive with an urban development organization. "But at this time, from talking to our members, we're seeing it as being manageable for this particular construction season."

Exhibit 5-3 Net Migration, 2014–2018, by City

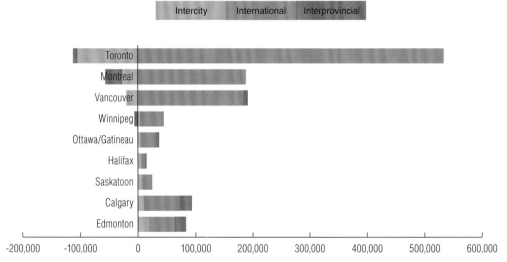

Source: Canadian Conference Board.

Indeed, the labor market is an area of concern across Canada, since there may be a mismatch in some areas with unemployment and others that have a labor shortage. The nation's skilled tradespeople and others are heading west for lucrative opportunities. Yet many industries are finding it hard to find and keep the people they need.

Developers and investors alike are also wary of rising government debt levels, especially at the provincial and municipal levels, and their impact on economic growth. Efforts to curb spending and reduce debt—while confronting a very real need for infrastructure investments—could have a significant effect on real estate markets. Transit investments, for example, open up attractive opportunities along new lines; however, rising development charges or other fees will continue to put pressure on pricing, which could cool development.

Demographics

Changes in Canadian demographics will make themselves felt in various real estate sectors. Employers will soon need to deal with a four-generation workforce, as generation Z joins the millennials, the middle-aged generation X, and a baby boomer cohort that is not quite ready to retire. Meeting their diverse and sometimes competing needs—from location and amenities to work style and office space preferences—could prove challenging both for employers and building owners alike.

Younger workers in particular—though not exclusively—continue to flock to the urban core, preferring to work where they live rather than take on long commutes. This continuing urbanization trend has fueled the condo boom in Toronto and other cities, but some question what will happen as the lifestyles of today's young urban singles and couples change. Will they move out of the city core in search of larger homes, schools, and services, or will they—like their counterparts in other parts of the world—simply adapt to smaller living spaces?

The movement of workers is driving location decisions for many employers. The recent surge in office construction in a number of markets is being driven to facilitate companies' ability to attract and retain qualified workers. Urbanization is creating greater demand for offices in downtown cores. This will result in increased vacancies in existing office space in the downtown cores, at least in the near term, as landlords seek to upgrade or reposition this space. It is also expected to put even more pressure on vacancies in suburban office spaces as more tenants move to the downtown core. While the move to the urban core is more visible, choosing the proper location is also important in the suburbs. Interviewees commented that any new development or redevelopment in the suburbs will be aimed at making it convenient for workers to get to the office. An interviewee noted, "People want to live mid-downtown. The subway/transit corridor is golden for developers."

Exhibit 5-4 **Housing Affordability**

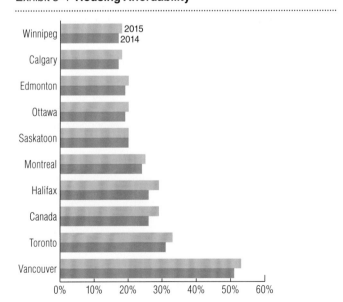

Source: *Quarterly Regional Housing Report*, July 3, 2014, TD Economics.

Note: Affordability is measured by the mortgage payment as a percentage of average household income. Mortgage payment is based on the average home price, 25 percent downpayment, 25-year amortization, and five-year fixed posted rate.

Exhibit 5-5 **Average Home Size, by Country**

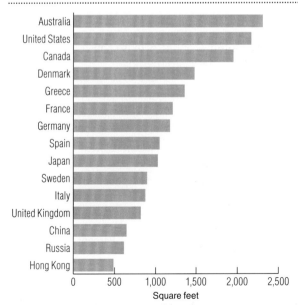

Sources: CommSec, Reserve Bank of Australia, United Nations, U.S. Census Bureau.

A more pressing concern is whether young families will be able to afford single-family homes at all. If baby boomers opt to stay in their homes rather than sell them, the market for detached single-family homes will only tighten. And as the supply of lots available for new detached single-family homes dwindles, particularly in Ontario given the Greenbelt legislation put in place a decade ago, prices will only continue to rise—beyond the reach of ever more Canadians. We may also see an increase in the number of multigenerational homes in the years to come as a result.

Emerging Trends in Canadian Real Estate

Canada's real estate market remains steady as the industry looks ahead to 2015. Economic growth in western Canada will continue to drive significant opportunity in Vancouver, Calgary, Edmonton, and Saskatoon in the residential, commercial, and office sectors. Despite continuing and ongoing concerns about overvaluation, Toronto's housing market continues as a solid performer, while office and industrial sectors remain strong. Montreal looks to revitalize its treasured retail district to boost an increasingly condo-driven core. In Atlantic Canada, Halifax will build up commercial and office space while hoping for the residential market's sluggishness to end. And everywhere, industry players will search for opportunities in and around the city cores—capitalizing on the trends of urbanization and reverse-migration that show little sign of abating.

Commercial and Residential Development Converges

Urbanization has become part of the new normal of Canadian real estate, rather than an emerging trend itself. Now, urbanization is sparking new trends that are blurring the lines between residential and commercial developers. An interviewee summed it up thusly: "Business overlap will increase and will drive behavioral changes—growth by intensification."

As many urban dwellers have discovered, services and amenities haven't kept up with the pace of downtown development—not only in terms of retail, but also health care, education, and other areas. In response, residential developers have begun to add retail and other services to their projects in a bid to attract buyers. At the same time, many commercial developers are adding a residential component to their office and retail projects. A major retailer, for example, recently signed a deal to develop land near one of its shopping centers into a high-rise residential complex. Other commercial property owners, including some real estate investment trusts (REITs), are redeveloping or intensifying existing properties to reflect mixed uses—usually with a residential component.

This convergence of commercial and residential development appears to be driven by a desire for developers to maximize upside by controlling more aspects of a project, to add value to their property holdings, and to grow. Some developers may encounter challenges as they cross over into less familiar ground, but we expect this trend to continue.

Looking ahead, we can expect to see more and more retail and services along the streets of Canada's city cores and along major transit arteries, especially where new developments predominate. Major brands are likely to move into these new spaces, too—though with new formats and smaller footprints. If done correctly, the addition of retail, services, and perhaps office space will create a positive synergy where each use provides customers or tenants for the other.

Office Tenants Demand New Space

Office tenants are demanding new amenities from builders in order to deliver the workspace configurations and features needed to attract and retain today's talent. New supply will be delivered in a number of markets as a result.

Market demand for this space is obvious, as a significant amount of this new space is preleased: Tenants appear quite willing to pay for the higher-quality space in many markets, so the new developments make good, long-term economic sense from the developers' perspective. Part of the economic decision is related to using less space per worker. Tenants may be

Table 5-3 **Downtown Class A Office Space: 2014**

Downtown	Under construction		Market vacancy rate	Proposed development (sq ft)
	Space (sq ft)	Percent preleased		
Toronto	5,000,000	56%	5.7%	5,700,000
Calgary	4,900,000	75%	2.5%	3,300,000
Vancouver	2,100,000	60%	5.9%	3,000,000
Montreal	1,100,000	58%	9.4%	4,800,000

Source: *The Canadian Quartet: Look Forward*, Summer 2014, Jones Lang LaSalle.

paying more per foot for the new space, but the impact on real estate costs is not a one-for-one exchange.

The leasing of the new space is no longer simply a real estate decision. The human resource department also is now often involved, as the quality and location of new space are seen as a very important tool to attract and retain talent.

The real impact of this new supply on the office market involves the space left behind as tenants move into their new space. Some older buildings will likely be upgraded to better compete with the newer spaces, while others will instead choose to compete on price, positioning older buildings as a lower-cost alternative for tenants who want a desirable location but who don't need all of the amenities offered by the new space. An interviewee put it well with the following quote: "*Tout le monde veut aller au ciel, mais personne ne veut mourir.*" Translated, everyone wants to go to heaven, but nobody wants to die. A number of office tenants want new office space, but may not be willing to pay the higher rents required. The result is that there is going to be a period of adjustment in these markets, when more space competes for changing composition of tenants.

While the interest in leasing the new space indicates that the market will welcome the new office space, there is no getting around the fact that it will cause some uncertainty in the affected office markets. Vacancy rates may increase and market rent is likely to become dynamic in a number of areas. One of our interviewees, a top real estate service provider, offered up his opinion on market rents: "There are really about four different market rents today. It all depends on the situation and the current status of the space." Different lease rates are being quoted for first-generation space, turnkey sublet space, vacant sublet space, and renewal rates.

The Rise of the "Superprime" Asset Class

So-called superprime assets continue to attract capital looking for safe returns. Superprime assets are defined as those whose location is considered irreplaceable. The use in these locations may change with market demand, but the actual physical and perhaps historical position of the property is unique. Since this type of asset is in short supply, the competition to purchase it can be intense. The level of competition leads to very aggressive pricing. An increasing number of investors are sitting on increasing levels of capital and are eager to put it to work in the perceived safety of these premium properties.

In Canada, the "flight to quality" has compelled investors to trade these irreplaceable assets at the lowest cap rates. The search for

high-quality assets is likely to continue; but with a limited supply and owners typically looking to hold for a longer term, future activity will be limited. They just don't trade very often.

The Pursuit of Assets Remains Intense—and Increasingly Global

Competition for high-quality Canadian assets is poised to intensify over the next few years.

Some real estate players are concerned that an influx of new foreign investors could drive Canada's already lofty valuations even higher and give rise to an asset bubble. However, Canada has one of the lowest proportions of foreign real estate investment in the world, and the domestic market is dominated by pension funds, insurers, and REITs. These domestic players have ample resources and a clear desire to increase their real estate holdings to secure strong returns in a secure environment. One interviewee put it this way: "Pension funds are pounding down the door to get into the pipeline for mixed-use projects." In addition, these players' knowledge of local markets may continue to give them the edge in winning key Canadian assets.

While valuations on prime assets are being pushed up by this competition, it's not a trend that's causing much concern in the market. Interviewees noted that the premium being paid for the best assets is not spreading to lower-quality assets in less desirable locations. The higher perceived risk is being appropriately reflected in cap rates.

Scarcity of Multiresidential Rental Assets Gives Rise to Development/Redevelopment Trend

Everyone, it seems, wants to be in the multiresidential rental sector—and the desire to hold on to these precious properties has resulted in a distinct lack of product on the market. With few opportunities to buy, companies are focusing instead on creating value from within their existing portfolios, often through development or redevelopment. These projects may well include purchasing existing assets to hold for potential redevelopment at a future date.

Developing multiresidential versus acquiring may also be an opportunity in this market. An interviewee mentioned that the combination of low interest rates and the potential for a reduced construction premium might make development returns more attractive than those that can be earned by acquiring high-priced assets. These opportunities may be limited, but could be worth exploring in 2015. Due to the age of the existing rental stock, the end result could be a portfolio of newer assets than what could be acquired in the market.

Table 5-4 Prime Multiresidential Rental Market, by Year of Construction

	Total	Before 1960	1960–1979	1980–1999	2000 or later
Quebec	779,011	316,317	290,457	119,931	52,306
Ontario	664,776	135,094	431,670	71,962	26,050
British Columbia	176,635	24,690	112,745	28,096	11,104
Alberta	131,185	7,766	85,027	25,484	12,908
Manitoba	61,891	12,860	35,072	7,720	6,239
Nova Scotia	52,499	7,577	20,067	13,633	11,222
Saskatchewan	34,392	4,303	20,519	7,381	2,189
New Brunswick	32,029	8,036	11,309	6,080	6,604
Prince Edward Island	6,400	1,447	1,025	2,298	1,630
Newfoundland/Labrador	5,680	1,223	2,721	1,206	530
Canada total	**1,946,443**	**519,336**	**1,011,298**	**284,556**	**131,253**

Source: CMHC Rental Market Survey.

Matching Lenders with Borrowers

The continuing flood of new capital into the Canadian real estate market, whether debt or equity, has also brought with it new and, in some cases, inexperienced lenders. There is a lot of competition to place capital, and this is being reflected in narrowing spreads and more favorable terms being reported by some of our interviewees. On the positive side, builders who are having trouble getting financed by traditional lenders may very well have alternative sources to consider. However, this may well put some of these new lenders in situations where they may find themselves involved with inexperienced developers. One interviewee remarked, "If a builder can't get bank financing, there is still capital available, but it does make you wonder about the potential viability of the project when you have two inexperienced parties involved." The resulting new product may not in fact be good for the local market, particularly in the condo sector.

The Continuation of Office Compression

Workplace location and quality are key tools that companies have used to attract and retain high-quality talent, and in recent years many companies have embraced open, collaborative work environments in order to engage younger workers. The result is more collaborative and flexible space along with examples of no offices, just work locations. But as the millennials get older and a new generation enters the workplace, will their tastes change—and will today's open, densely populated offices be what the market demands? The rise in workspace flexibility could help deal with any change in space demand per worker. Today's new flexible workspace could be adjusted to meet new worker configurations.

Rising Construction Costs: Hindrance or Benefit?

The ongoing battle for talent between the real estate construction sector and Canada's booming natural resources industry continues to drive up labor costs. At the same time, continued Asian demand for construction materials is boosting real estate input costs. Many industry watchers fear this could slow down the pace of development—or even stop projects from getting off the ground. Yet others see rising costs as a means to avoid overbuilding.

Exhibit 5-6 Inflation and Interest Rate Changes

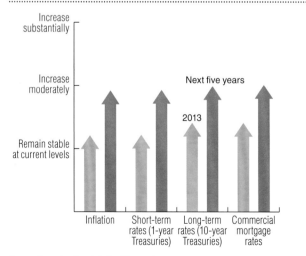

Source: *Emerging Trends in Real Estate 2015* survey.

Note: Based on Canadian investors only.

Exhibit 5-7 Real Estate Capital Market Balance Forecast

Debt capital for acquisitions

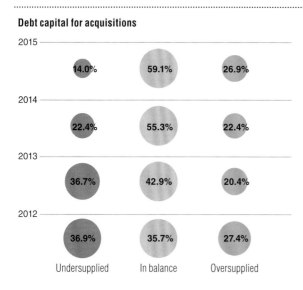

Debt capital for refinancing

Debt capital for development

Source: *Emerging Trends in Real Estate* surveys.
Note: Based on Canadian investors only.

Exhibit 5-8 Real Estate Capital Market Balance Forecast

Equity capital for investing

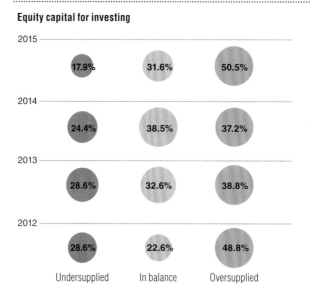

Source: *Emerging Trends in Real Estate* surveys.
Note: Based on Canadian investors only.

Municipal Issues

Municipal government policy plays an influential—and, in many cases, frustrating—role in real estate development across Canada. Interviewees noted that limited land being made available as well as increasingly lengthy and costly approval processes are areas of concern with municipal governments.

As residents and businesses alike strive to make their voices heard at the municipal level, it may well be time for the real estate industry to do the same, especially around urban issues. Interviewees commented that a great opportunity exists for real estate industry associations to play an important advocacy role on many urban issues, especially around planning, zoning, and transit. A prime example would be encouraging more multiuse zoning, to allow developers to combine residential, retail, and other services (e.g., medical clinics) and create the vibrant urban cores people demand.

Is Consolidation in the Cards for Canadian Real Estate Owners?

With Canada's limited stock of investable properties—and the market flooded with capital and low-cost debt—is some industry consolidation in the cards? It could become increasingly difficult for all market participants to continue to grow. Will smaller players be able to access the capital and find investment opportunities to support continued growth? Or could we see firms opt for growth through a merger with or acquisition of other market participants? Consolidation may be a way for real estate companies to expand their opportunities for growth by expanding into new areas of expertise or getting access to new development projects.

Capital Markets

The consensus view among real estate players is that interest rates will rise at some point, but any move is unlikely to occur until the second half of 2015 at the earliest. Interviewees expressed confidence that increased capacity worldwide is limiting any upward pressure on interest rates. The improvement in the U.S. economy indicates that higher rates could be coming, but the economic stability in Canada and the United States will continue to attract foreign capital. In addition, retiring baby boomers are likely to flood the market with private capital as they look to turn stock options and retirement packages into stable, income-generating assets.

Investors operating on shorter time horizons will be less concerned with the direction of rates, but longer-term players will want to factor the impact of higher rates into pricing and net operating income. We can expect to see larger players continue to prune and refocus their portfolios in the years ahead, and sell some secondary market properties or those that don't currently align with their portfolio strategy. Shorter-term investors and those looking to grow their portfolios will be keen to snap up these properties.

A lot of debt will be coming due over the next couple of years. Many companies face an elevated debt maturity schedule because it was very difficult to secure longer-term debt in the aftermath of the financial crisis. With rates remaining low, we

Exhibit 5-9 **Global Capital Flows**

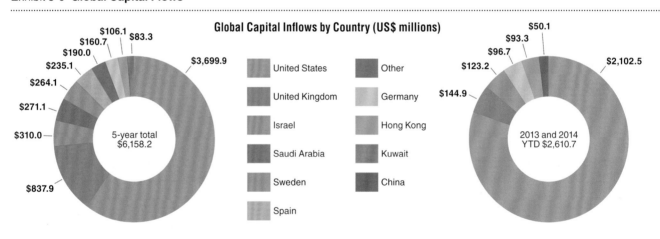

Source: Real Capital Analytics.

Exhibit 5-10 **Equity Underwriting Standards Forecast for Canada**

	Less rigorous	Remain the same	More rigorous
2015	24.5%	55.3%	20.2%
2014	11.5%	44.8%	43.7%
2013	6.7%	51.1%	42.2%
2012	7.8%	54.9%	37.2%

Source: *Emerging Trends in Real Estate 2015* survey.
Note: Based on Canadian investors only.

Exhibit 5-11 **Debt Underwriting Standards Forecast for Canada**

	Less rigorous	Remain the same	More rigorous
2015	25.8%	57.0%	17.2%
2014	9.5%	40.5%	50.0%
2013	5.9%	45.1%	49.0%
2012	6.6%	34.1%	59.3%

Source: *Emerging Trends in Real Estate 2015* survey.
Note: Based on Canadian investors only.

can expect to see companies continuing to focus on refinancing their existing debt before rates start to rise in the future. Those market players looking for capital may have attractive options. A number of interviewees commented that debt capital is abundant and typically available in Canada at 65 to 70 percent of the value on income property. Canadian financing of up to 85 percent on developments is available, though syndication is often required once deals reach a certain size. Construction financing for condo projects remains available, but the primary lenders continue to focus their lending on established builders with healthy balance sheets. Others will have to look to the many alternative lenders in or entering the market.

Fortunately, most market participants feel that debt capital will continue to be readily available in 2015. This increase in capital availability should be able to absorb the amount of debt maturing. Debt capital will be available, but lenders will remain diligent in their underwriting criteria.

REITs

Stable cap rates allowed the majority of REITs to avoid a significant decrease in property values. Further cap-rate compression is likely to be limited in 2015, and this will make it difficult to find investments that meet the current yield requirements. Delivering growth and value will have to be earned the old-fashioned way, through growth in net operating income and improved quality of cash flows instead of relying on continued cap-rate compression. A number of REITs have already identified this market reality and have begun actively increasing development and redevelopment activity to enhance the value of existing properties and have identified development pipelines that will take place over the next several years.

Some REITs continue to trade below their net asset values, prompting some interviewees to speculate that we could see some takeovers or mergers if the unit prices soften further. One industry executive remarked, "There are a number of organiza-

tions, both public and private, that are identifying their targets, they're doing their homework, and they're preparing should the REIT market continue to weaken." In addition, there have been a large number of new entrants over the last two years, and most of them are at the lower end of the market capitalization. There will be pressure for them to grow their portfolios or take some actions to contain their cost structures. One REIT executive feels that "new REITs may need to merge to get to critical mass, but being externally managed they are not really incentivized to do so." The market may see increased investor/unit-holder activism to force consolidation.

The larger, established Canadian REITs appear to be evolving to more of a U.S. REIT model with lower debt-to-equity ratios and lower payout ratios focused more on total return rather than just returning a certain yield target. Initial public offering (IPO) activity is expected to be down in 2015 as any new entrant needs to have a significant story to be successful. REITs, generally, have underperformed, making it more difficult to attract new equity capital. Investors are choosing alternative investments that offer a more intriguing growth story. In response, some REITs and real estate operating companies (REOCs) have been looking to intensification and redevelopment of their existing properties in order to drive value in their portfolios.

Consolidation may also be driven by pension funds and others looking to increase their real estate allocations. A limited amount of private market investments could make acquiring a REIT and its portfolio an attractive alternative. REITs, meanwhile, are likely to sell off some of their noncore assets as they increasingly focus on improving their current real estate portfolios and developing new properties. One real estate analyst expressed the opinion that "real estate companies with a focus on development and redevelopment growth strategies—as opposed to REITs that strictly buy existing properties—are more likely to outperform going forward."

Banks

Canadian banks remain active but discerning real estate lenders. Banks continue to aggressively pursue high-quality commercial real estate projects, and continue to provide capital to low-rise residential development. They continue to be cautious regarding high-rise residential development, opting only to fund projects with established borrowers. Foreign banks and alternative lenders, armed with lots of capital, also are aggressively looking for opportunities, but are finding it hard to identify places to make loans.

Underwriting remains strict and disciplined, with a focus on blue-chip opportunities; there is no sign that underwriting standards are shifting in response to banks' desire to get more money working in the sector. Banks remain insistent on seeing real estate players put more equity into any deal and taking a careful look at project budgets before approving loans. This desire to put money to work in the market prompted one interviewee to comment: "Loan sizes are on the rise. Larger loans are now possible without requiring syndication—at least on good deals that have developer equity, solid covenants, and a good project plan in place. Construction loans are being made available at 80 percent to 85 percent of project value."

Mezzanine and Equity Financing

The flow of mezzanine and equity dollars into Canadian real estate will increase in 2015. One interviewee noted, "Pension funds have increased their real estate asset allocation in recent years, and now look to have larger percentages of their portfolios in real estate." The abundance of funds available means that investors are putting money into the market at very low returns.

Large pension and investment funds remain a major source of these funds. However, interest from investors in the United States, Israel, the U.K., and Saudi Arabia also is bringing more money into the market. Many of these international investors are willing to accept modest returns in exchange for Canada's political and economic stability.

Canadian investors aren't confining themselves to the domestic market, however. Canadian funds will continue to flow outward, into high-quality real estate properties around the world and in jurisdictions such as London, New York, Ireland, and Malaysia, which offer tax advantages. Canada continues to be the leading nondomestic investor in U.S. real estate by a substantial margin. This trend is likely to continue, but Canadian investors will also keep looking for investments in Mexico and Latin America.

Exhibit 5-12 Prospects for Commercial/Multifamily Subsectors in 2015

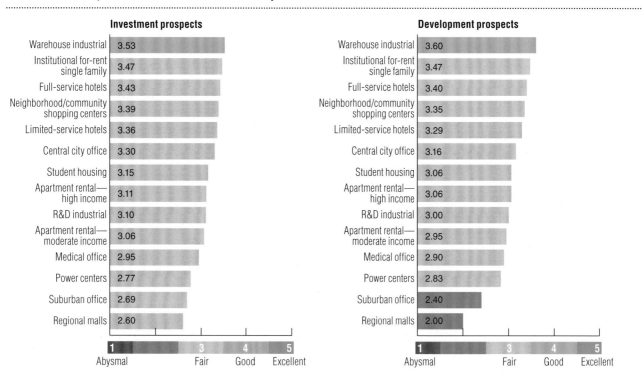

Investment prospects		Development prospects	
Warehouse industrial	3.53	Warehouse industrial	3.60
Institutional for-rent single family	3.47	Institutional for-rent single family	3.47
Full-service hotels	3.43	Full-service hotels	3.40
Neighborhood/community shopping centers	3.39	Neighborhood/community shopping centers	3.35
Limited-service hotels	3.36	Limited-service hotels	3.29
Central city office	3.30	Central city office	3.16
Student housing	3.15	Student housing	3.06
Apartment rental—high income	3.11	Apartment rental—high income	3.06
R&D industrial	3.10	R&D industrial	3.00
Apartment rental—moderate income	3.06	Apartment rental—moderate income	2.95
Medical office	2.95	Medical office	2.90
Power centers	2.77	Power centers	2.83
Suburban office	2.69	Suburban office	2.40
Regional malls	2.60	Regional malls	2.00

1 Abysmal   3 Fair   4 Good   5 Excellent

Source: *Emerging Trends in Real Estate 2015* survey.

Note: Based on Canadian investors only.

Exhibit 5-13 Prospects for Major Commercial Property Types, 2015 versus 2014

Investment prospects

	2015	2014
Industrial	3.47	3.22
Hotel	3.43	2.46
Apartment	3.28	3.31
Office	2.96	3.17
Retail	2.87	3.37

Development prospects

	2015	2014
Industrial	3.40	3.18
Apartment	3.28	3.02
Hotel	3.00	2.36
Office	2.80	2.93
Retail	2.60	3.13

1	2	3	4	5
Abysmal	Poor	Fair	Good	Excellent

Source: *Emerging Trends in Real Estate* surveys.

Note: Based on Canadian investors only.

Exhibit 5-14 Retail Investment Prospects

Neighborhood/community centers

2015	Prospects	Rating	Ranking
Investment	3.39	Fair	4
Development	3.35	Fair	4

Buy 40.6%	Hold 37.5%	Sell 21.9%

Expected capitalization rate, December 2015: 6.4%

Power centers

2015	Prospects	Rating	Ranking
Investment	2.77	Fair	12
Development	2.40	Poor	13

Buy 18.8%	Hold 25.0%	Sell 56.3%

Expected capitalization rate, December 2015: 6.4%

Regional malls

2015	Prospects	Rating	Ranking
Investment	2.60	Fair	14
Development	2.00	Poor	14

Buy 25.0%	Hold 28.1%	Sell 46.9%

Expected capitalization rate, December 2015: 6.0%

Source: *Emerging Trends in Real Estate 2015* survey.

Note: Based on Canadian investors only.

Opportunities by Property Type

The 2015 survey respondents matched the views of this year's interviewees. The outlook for the office and retail sectors declined from 2014. Survey respondents have recognized the challenges that both market sectors will be facing.

The apartment and industrial sectors, however, were viewed more favorably than in 2014. The opportunity spotted by survey participants echoes the comments of interviewees who like the potential for investment and development in these property types.

Retail

The retail market remains bifurcated at a number of levels. There is a distinct difference in performance by location, format, and retailer. Interviewees feel good about the outlook for the urban core in Greater Toronto and Calgary, prompting one interviewee to summarize these markets as "a tale of two cities." Established malls and new urban formats seem attractive, while less competi-

tive strip malls and power centers struggle as consumer tastes take them in a different direction. Finally, retailers at the luxury level and those that meet convenience needs are doing well, while the commodity retailers struggle with new competition.

Despite the challenges, one interviewee noted that shopping centers are still the cheapest form of distribution. Shopping malls also have a social aspect to them: "The demise of shopping centers and malls is fiction." Shopping centers remain the most hands-on way to get products to customers.

E-commerce, mobile technology, and changing consumer behaviors and expectations continue to transform the retail sector, and this is having a knock-on effect in real estate. As consumers embrace showrooming and online purchases, retailers are reconsidering the role of the store and exploring new formats and footprints as a result. With physical stores playing a less central role in the shopping experience, landlords in some markets are losing pricing power and can't dictate the number and location of storefronts as they did in the past.

With few good locations for new retail, developers are instead focusing on existing assets. Some are adding more space for retail and services in residential or commercial properties, while others are considering adding a residential or office component to retail properties. Urban retail is set to see strong growth, as the influx of residents to city cores drives up demand for amenities. Mixed-use properties will become increasingly common.

Power centers have been especially hard hit by competition from online retailers, and this market is flat or declining across the country—though centers anchored by grocery stores or pharmacies are still proving viable for the moment. Demand remains strong for fashion-focused centers, however.

Retail outlet developments appear to be here to stay—and grow. "Off-price is the 'in thing,' " remarked one interviewee. "It's scary to see how much stuff is sold, and how much people like outlets." Outlet centers continue to lure busloads of shoppers each day—and these shoppers come determined to buy something to justify the trip.

Purpose-Built Multiresidential Rental Properties

With home prices rising and people keen to be close to the urban core, some developers are discovering opportunities in purpose-built multiresidential development or redevelopment. Increasing location density, or adding a retail component to the mix, could prove key to making the economics work.

Investors also are taking interest in multiresidential properties, seeing them as a way to lock in income and potentially realize significant upside at the end of the term. Patience will be key: rent controls and other factors may put some limits on the returns that investors can expect, and "making the numbers work" is still project-specific. Rental projects may also require significant amounts of ongoing investment to keep the product quality at a level where it can compete with rental stock represented by newer condos.

Single-Family Homes

Canada's housing market remains largely buoyant and housing prices remain high. Land prices, development charges, and labor costs are contributing factors, as are a number of other trends. Buyers are using existing home equity to move up into pricier homes. Parents are helping their children get into the property market. Family members abroad are helping Canadian relatives by shifting money into the country. Immigration continues to have an impact on the Canadian economy. Immigration

Exhibit 5-15 Apartment Investment Prospects

Apartments—high income

2015	Prospects	Rating	Ranking
Investment	3.11	Fair	8
Development	3.47	Fair	2

Buy 30.0%	Hold 35.0%	Sell 35.0%

Expected capitalization rate, December 2015: 5.2%

Apartments—moderate income

2015	Prospects	Rating	Ranking
Investment	3.06	Fair	10
Development	3.06	Fair	8

Buy 40.0%	Hold 32.5%	Sell 27.5%

Expected capitalization rate, December 2015: 5.9%

Source: *Emerging Trends in Real Estate 2015* survey.
Note: Based on Canadian investors only.

into Canada, between provinces, and within cities will have an impact on labor markets and could contribute to upward pressure on home prices.

Housing affordability continues to be a topic of concern and conversation. Many industry watchers worry about the impact of rising rates on the market for single-family homes—and as we've seen, most expect rates to rise at least somewhat in the near term. Others believe that the inflow of foreign money and a scarcity of appropriate sites for new development will keep prices rising. In addition to helping with affordability, municipalities welcome mid-rise development as it assists them in meeting their intensification quotas. However, this may be at odds with consumer demand and developer wishes in some areas.

Looking ahead, our interviewees indicate that it's likely that we will see at least some drop-off in large tower residential. Instead, it's anticipated that mid-rise developments—which are subject to lower development charges—will become more popular, particularly in the suburbs and in core infill projects.

Exhibit 5-16 Industrial Investment Prospects

Warehouse industrial

2015	Prospects	Rating	Ranking
Investment	3.53	Good	1
Development	3.60	Good	1

Buy 64.5%		Hold 35.5%

Expected capitalization rate, December 2015:   5.8%

R&D industrial

2015	Prospects	Rating	Ranking
Investment	3.10	Fair	9
Development	3.06	Fair	7

Buy 24.1%	Hold 44.8%	Sell 31.0%

Expected capitalization rate, December 2015:   6.8%

Source: *Emerging Trends in Real Estate 2015* survey.
Note: Based on Canadian investors only.

Seniors' Housing

Canada's aging population means that seniors' housing offers some attractive opportunities in the years ahead, and serves as an alternative multiresidential investment. Vacancy rates are low and returns can be quite strong in some instances. Some investors may choose to partner with firms specializing in facility management, rather than take on operational matters themselves. And companies should take into account the important differences between independent-living facilities and long-term care or convalescence properties, as the returns can be quite different.

Industrial

The industrial market is performing well, fueled by a rise in single-tenant big-box developments designed for distribution. An industrial investor summarized the trend in the market thusly: "Industrial is transformational. The days of the small-bay, multi-tenant building are waning. We are now seeing new 200,000- to 500,000-square-foot buildings with larger bays." Despite this transformation, the outlook for older, smaller industrial space is being helped as companies look to augment their local distribution capabilities at lower costs. Redevelopment opportunities will emerge in the industrial market as developers look to upgrade sites for industrial companies or "retool" for other uses. With land scarce and expensive, we may eventually see the rise of multilevel industrial properties.

Exhibit 5-17 Office Investment Prospects

Central city office

2015	Prospects	Rating	Ranking
Investment	3.30	Fair	6
Development	2.95	Fair	10

Buy 50.0%	Hold 27.3%	Sell 22.7%

Expected capitalization rate, December 2015:   5.9%

Suburban office

2015	Prospects	Rating	Ranking
Investment	2.69	Fair	13
Development	2.83	Fair	12

Buy 22.7%	Hold 15.9%	Sell 61.4%

Expected capitalization rate, December 2015:   5.2%

Medical office

2015	Prospects	Rating	Ranking
Investment	2.95	Fair	11
Development	2.90	Fair	11

Buy 17.1%	Hold 63.4%	Sell 19.5%

Expected capitalization rate, December 2015:   6.5%

Source: *Emerging Trends in Real Estate 2015* survey.
Note: Based on Canadian investors only.

Office Space

The outlook for office space depends very much on location. In the urban core, tenants' desire to use space efficiently, be close to their workers, and deliver the amenities those workers want is driving the demand for new and upgraded space. These new spaces are leasing quickly as tenants move from their older offices; however, it is unclear who will move into the space they have vacated.

The rise in the use of technology to facilitate how work gets done is a key component of new office demand. The new space being delivered is capable of providing ongoing flexibility and further implementation of new technology. Owners of older office space will find it necessary to decide whether to invest the capital in their properties to provide these same amenities or find another way to compete for tenants.

The overall view among this year's interviewees is that suburban office space will continue to be challenged in 2015. With most activity in this sector focused on urban centers, interviewees see limited opportunities in the suburbs. One interviewee, however, sees the potential for suburban office properties along key transit lines—and should urban congestion worsen, we may see companies opt to establish offices outside the core in order to better serve workers who wish to avoid arduous commutes. Some non-core located building landlords are being creative to make their buildings more attractive by adding private bus services for tenants' employees to link to transit hubs and avoid over-crowded public buses and streetcars.

Medical Offices

In medical office space, the clear trend is away from the old sole-practitioner model to multifunctional, multiphysician clinics offering longer hours and a wider range of services. At the same time, small facilities—laboratories, for example—will likely look to consolidate in order to control costs and achieve economies of scale. Hospitals also will look to move some services such as rehabilitation out of their main facilities into other, less expensive locations.

Property owners and developers may find themselves facing the need to move tenants out of existing assets in order to secure the space needed for these new clinics—or they may look for opportunities to develop or redevelop other properties to suit.

The opportunities are greatest in western Canada, where the population is rising and many residents are young families with

children. In addition, stronger provincial balance sheets are allowing governments to invest more money into local health care. The chief problem in the west, of course, is that land is very expensive.

In Ontario and Quebec, by contrast, we will see health care spending cut back as governments wrestle with budget deficits. These spending reductions may put pressures on space demand and consequently medical property valuations.

Markets to Watch in 2015

The economic strength of the western portion of Canada is reflected in the 2015 survey respondents' market rankings. Survey respondents were asked to rank each market on the potential for 2015 commercial investment, development and the strength of the housing market. The rankings range from 1 = abysmal to 5 = excellent. Calgary and Edmonton are again the top two markets, scoring well for investment, development, and housing. Toronto slips in just ahead of Vancouver to hold the number-three rank in this year's survey. The rankings reflect the overall strength of the markets with all markets in the fair range, and the majority either higher in the fair or good range.

Exhibit 5-18 Markets to Watch: Overall Real Estate Prospects

	Investment	Development	Housing
1 Calgary (1/3/1)	3.42	3.40	4.00
2 Edmonton (3/1/4)	3.37	3.53	3.64
3 Toronto (5/2/2)	3.29	3.41	3.83
4 Vancouver (4/5/5)	3.34	3.33	3.56
5 Ottawa (2/4/6)	3.37	3.39	3.13
6 Montreal (8/8/3)	2.98	2.93	3.75
7 Winnipeg (7/7/6)	3.10	3.09	3.13
8 Saskatoon (6/6/9)	3.15	3.15	2.50
9 Halifax (9/9/8)	2.83	2.83	3.00

1		3	4	5
Abysmal		Fair	Good	Excellent

Source: *Emerging Trends in Real Estate 2015* survey.
Note: Based on Canadian investors only.

Calgary

- Strongest market in the country.

- Robust office growth amid developer confidence.

- Housing starts struggle due to rising costs.

Calgary remains the strongest market in Canada. Employment continues to rise, with over 28,000 jobs created in the past year and the unemployment rate holding steady at 5.4 percent.

The city has become a hotbed of office construction. More than 7 million square feet of office space has been built in the past five years—and another 5 million square feet is under construction or in design. Demand for this new space is high: nearly two-thirds of future downtown office inventory is preleased, and over half of the inventory along the Beltline and in suburban markets is preleased.

While the new development is being driven by tenant demand, the market will likely go through a period of adjustment as tenants exit existing locations. It will take time for the vacated space to lease back up. Another concern in the Calgary market is the potential for a cyclical downturn in the resource industry. The majority of the new demand is coming from this industry, and several interviewees expressed concern about market impact if natural resource prices were to fall significantly.

On the other hand, getting houses built has become extraordinarily difficult. There simply isn't the manpower, and the municipal government's decision to focus growth in the northeast and southeast of the city is limiting the availability of lots and pushing up prices. Many housing developers are instead choosing to build outside Calgary in communities such as Airdrie, Chestermere, and Okotoks, which are actively encouraging development.

Like other Canadian cities, Calgary is experiencing its own urban densification (though unlike its counterparts, it continues to see development at the city edges). The millions of square feet of new office space coming on stream in the years ahead will accommodate 40,000 workers, many of whom will wish to live downtown. As a consequence, Calgary is seeing a downtown expansion with new master-planned urban villages under construction or in design around the traditional downtown area.

Construction has also begun on a number of condo projects that represents the first residential real estate development in the city's west end in several years. These projects are seen as a "significant milestone for the city that signals a shift toward urbanism . . . and is 60 percent presold," states an interviewee.

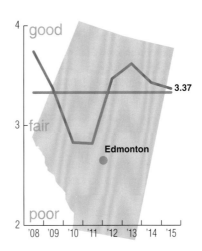

Edmonton

- Strong job creation.

- Lots of new development in the urban core.

- Worries over labor and material costs have yet to emerge.

Robust growth in residential construction, retail sales and personal services sectors is expected to assume a more prominent role in Edmonton's expansion of the next 12 to 24 months. These strong fundamental drivers will help insulate Edmonton's economy from external shocks.

The Edmonton economy is strong. Roughly 31,000 jobs were added over the past year, with unemployment edging up to a mere 5.5 percent. The economic table indicates a 2015 forecast of 4.8% in 2015. "Alberta's job market is operating in a different realm from the rest of the country," said an interviewee. The combination of big resource projects and the province's solid economic fundamentals is creating a "perfect storm for job creation now and in the foreseeable future."

Over the next five years, economic growth in Edmonton is expected to average 3.6 percent annually; in the Edmonton Census Metropolitan Area (CMA), 3.9 percent annually. The combination of relatively low interest rates and modest inflation over the next 12 to 24 months will sustain a very favorable environment for the city of Edmonton to undertake major capital investments. Low interest rates will help contain financing costs, while modest inflation will make estimates of final costs for multi-year projects much more reliable.

Edmonton is poised to benefit from improving economies in a number of major trading partners. Stronger economic growth in the United States could boost both commodity prices and lead to a higher level of Canadian exports. Emerging markets such as China and Brazil are expected to grow at respectable rates, which could increase demand for Canadian products. Growth in these countries may help offset expected weakness in the Eurozone economy.

The city is rife with new projects under construction or under development, from office towers and hotels to condominiums, a provincial museum, and a new downtown arena for the NHL's Edmonton Oilers. A number of construction firms report having work committed for the next two years.

The building boom is giving rise to fears that labor and material costs could jump. However, cost escalations and worker shortages haven't yet approached the peaks hit in the mid-2000s—in part because international construction activity isn't nearly as hectic, notes an interviewee.

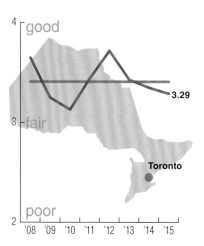

Toronto

- Condo market continues to be strong and stable.

- Affordable housing is a major concern that could spark multiresidential development.

- Retail is keen to move into the urban core at expense of suburbs.

- Suburban offices are in decline as businesses follow workers into the core.

In Toronto, the condo market remains strong, driven in part by the high cost of single-family homes in and around the core and a very robust condo rental market. However, prices are expected to remain relatively flat, and some industry watchers are voicing concerns about what happens as young urban condo-dwellers begin to start families. Most expect at least some residents to move out of the core in search of more—and more affordable—space. Yet they also foresee Toronto residents adapting to smaller spaces and family life in the urban core, much as their counterparts in London, New York, and other major cities have done.

Affordable housing is needed, especially for the city's "support network" of service industry workers. Purpose-built multiresidential rental developments are starting to address this market need.

In the office market, tenants continue to search for a way to reduce their office footprint, and many firms are moving into new properties in the core to do this. Like Vancouver, Toronto may struggle with re-leasing the space vacated as tenants move into new locations—a worry expressed by some observers. A number of interviewees feel that the ongoing migration of people and businesses back to the core will soak up the added capacity. The prevailing view is that the suburban office is in decline, a victim of the migration to the urban core.

Retail is expected to perform well in the core, as developers look for opportunities to provide residents with the services and amenities they demand. Multipurpose developments (or redevelopments) will become increasingly common as shops, clinics, restaurants, and other services transform condo developments into neighborhoods.

As the U.S. economy continues to improve and e-retailing continues to take hold, industry players are bullish on Greater Toronto's industrial space, especially space developed or redeveloped for distribution and logistics purposes—a sector that's an increasingly essential part of the retailing world as e-commerce continues to transform that business.

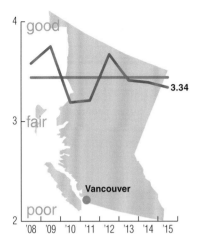

Vancouver

- Poised to lead Canada in economic growth.

- Foreign investment continues to keep housing prices high.

- New office construction stokes concerns over oversupply and downward price pressure.

After a lackluster 2013, Vancouver's economy appears to be turning a corner. Vancouver is expected to lead other major Canadian cities in growth in 2015, with local GDP rising 3.2 percent annually over the next three years, according to a spring 2014 Conference Board of Canada report. The same report forecasts unemployment falling from 6.2 percent today to 5 percent by 2018, due in no small part to a 1.5 percent rise in employment in 2014 and 2.6 percent growth in 2015. As well, Vancouverites' per-capita income is expected to rise from $41,000 to $48,000 by 2018—welcome news in a city with such sky-high housing costs.

Foreign buyers—the vast majority of whom hail from mainland China or Hong Kong—are, of course, one of the key reasons Vancouver real estate prices continue to rise. A 2013 report by Sotheby's International Realty Canada declares that foreign buyers account for about 40 percent of the demand for Vancouver's luxury single-family homes.

The reason for this is that Vancouver has become what one interviewee calls a "hedge city." Vancouver lacks the cultural cachet of Paris or Milan. But it does offer comfort and stability—and a place for the world's super-rich to park sizable funds in local real estate as a hedge against risk. Returns aren't the point; safety of capital is, and a C$5 million condo is more insurance policy than investment.

With a brighter economic future and a steady flow of foreign investment, it comes as little surprise that Vancouver issued a record number of building permits in the first year of 2014—C$1.12 billion, a figure not seen since the 2008 recession and a 6.7 percent increase over the same period last year.

Developers in Vancouver continue to deal with new Community Amenity Contribution requirements. The development community has developed an attitude that these "voluntary contributions" for rezoning projects have unofficially become mandatory in order to get projects approved. These contributions can greatly increase the cost and complexity of getting projects approved.

Not that there aren't concerns in the Vancouver market. Several new office towers are due to be completed in the next year or two, and industry watchers have expressed worries about the potential for overcapacity, a spike in vacancy rates, and downward pressure on price. Some foresee AAA space leasing at B rates, barring a significant boost to the economy—though progress on liquid natural gas projects or Northern Gateway could change the picture very rapidly.

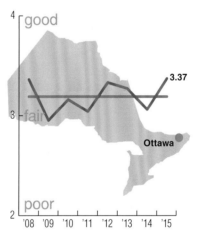

Ottawa

- LRT project is creating boom for local construction firms.

- Employment figures remain soft.

- Ottawa perceived as one of the best places to live in Canada.

The biggest story in Ottawa construction is the new Light Rail Transit (LRT) project. More than C$360 million in contracts have been committed to Ottawa firms so far, and the majority of contractors working on the downtown LRT tunnel and other first-phase projects are from the region. Construction of the 2.5-kilometer underground corridor—a key link in the overall project—was slated to reach the midway point by late summer 2014. Also underway is above-ground work to the east and west and a large maintenance facility.

That's welcome news to the National Capital Region, where the jobless rate rose to 6.8 percent in April 2014.

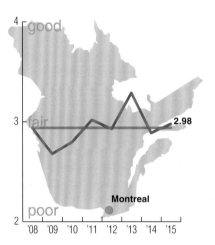

Montreal

● Office market likely to coast.

● Condo market takes a breather.

● Retail set for major overhaul as high-end retailers eye opportunities.

The Montreal market is viewed by interviewees as being stable. The transition from a manufacturing economy to one dominated by new-economy industries continues as the market continues to benefit from steady to growing employment in health care– and technology-related industries. As Montreal is home to several French and English universities as well as two new state-of-the-art hospitals, growth in these industries is likely to continue. In addition, the market should see a direct benefit from significant infrastructure investments over the next five years.

Not surprisingly, the office market in Montreal is expected to coast along in the year ahead, little changed from the previous year. Major office assets in Montreal are around 20 to 30 years old, though there are some smaller projects currently under development, including a number of office loft conversions. One major office project underway in the market near the "Quad Windsor" office/retail/residential development is planned next door to the Bell Centre, home of the Montreal Canadiens franchise. When finished, in 15 years, the project will cover 4.5 million square feet.

Montreal is experiencing its own migration back to the city core, primarily younger workers and retirees. After several years of elevated condo development, the market is expected to see a drop in activity in 2015 as the market continues to absorb the new inventory. Historically, Montreal residents have tended to prefer renting to owning, but the attraction of new condos along with favorable financing conditions is making condo living popular in the market. In an interesting contrast to condo markets in other Canadian cities, a majority of condos in Montreal are (or will be) owner-occupied.

The Montreal retail market is experiencing many of the same retail trends as the rest of the country. Depending on location, older big-box centers may be struggling. However, Montreal retail is expected to undergo a significant transformation in the downtown core. Montreal is keen to attract the sort of high-end retailers commonly found among the cores in other Canadian cities. Rue Ste. Catherine is "ground zero" for the city's retail ambitions, and most industry watchers expect the storied avenue to be utterly transformed over the next five years.

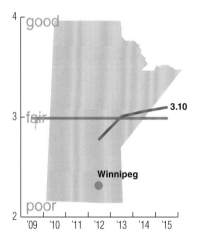

Winnipeg

● Home sales fall due to oversupply.

● Worries over overbuilding and impact on city finances and infrastructure.

● City is slated to get first power center.

"Softening demand due to lower employment and net immigration should keep housing starts below 2013 levels moving forward," said a senior market analyst for a Winnipeg real estate company. The market is currently dealing with a building up of unsold homes from 2013 and slower homebuying and building activity due to an unusually cold winter. New home construction had declined for the fourth straight month by March 2014, down 6.1 percent from the previous year.

Some feel the slowdown is necessary: Recently, the Manitoba Building and Construction Trades Council, which represents 13 construction and trade unions, called for a ten-year moratorium—if not longer—on major housing developments such as large-scale suburbs. The group believes that new developments are putting a serious financial strain on the city's budget and contributing to Winnipeg's growing infrastructure deficit. Others, including some in the city government, disagree, believing that new suburbs are essential to handling population growth and preventing people from leaving Winnipeg for surrounding bedroom communities.

Winnipeg shoppers are looking forward to the opening of the city's first pure outlet center. The Outlet Collection of Winnipeg will feature 90 premium retailers on a 40-acre site, and is anticipated to open in spring 2017. The project is expected to provide a strong boost to the local construction sector.

Buoyed by such "cautious optimism," Saskatoon housing sales are proceeding at a near-record pace. A local housing sales manager remarked, "The Saskatoon market is on track to easily record its second-highest volume ever for units sold." Prices, however, have risen only marginally in the first half of 2014. While sales have been very strong, inventory is at its highest point in five years.

New supply of industrial space has Saskatoon companies cheering. A local industrial service provider remarked: "There was a time, not so long ago, when our industrial vacancy rate was less than 2 percent and tenants were basically shoehorned into whatever building was available." Tenants often had to choose from a very short list of vacancies that might not have been the best fit for their operations.

With construction completed on a number of speculative projects in 2013—and more space expected to be delivered in 2014—industrial tenants looking to expand or relocate operations now have options.

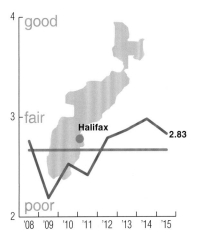

Saskatoon

- Optimism abounds among Saskatoon businesses.

- Home sales are at a near-record pace while prices rise slowly.

- Huge boost in speculative industrial space cheers companies.

Interviewees expressed optimism about Saskatoon. This feeling is attributed to the outlook for future business growth that is expected to increase the level of capital investment in the city and lead to the hiring of additional workers.

Halifax

- Housing sales hit a 19-year low amid oversupply, a downsizing trend, stubborn prices, and mortgage rule changes.

- Head/regional offices and new industry concentrations boosting office construction.

- Industrial market wavers as shipbuilding fails to deliver anticipated jobs.

Economic and job-related uncertainty is dampening confidence in the Halifax housing market. Sales of existing homes hit a 19-year low in the first quarter of 2014, according to an RBC Economic Research report. The housing sales drop is due to

Table 5-5 Survey Participants' View of Their Local Market

	Strength of local economy	Investor demand	Capital availability	Development/ redevelopment opportunities	Public/private investment	Local development community
Calgary	4.87	4.93	4.71	4.46	4.33	4.08
Edmonton	4.64	4.62	4.54	4.25	4.58	4.08
Vancouver	3.77	4.50	4.43	3.69	3.38	3.85
Saskatoon	3.67	3.67	3.67	4.00	4.00	3.67
Toronto	3.61	4.17	4.18	3.64	3.82	4.23
Halifax	3.50	3.00	3.25	3.00	3.00	3.67
Ottawa	3.17	3.00	3.83	3.40	3.20	3.60
Winnipeg	3.17	3.33	3.17	3.00	3.17	3.00
Montreal	3.00	3.50	3.50	3.33	2.89	3.44

Source: *Emerging Trends in Real Estate 2015* survey.

Note: Based on Canadian investors only.

several factors, including oversupply, a downsizing trend, stubbornly high prices, and recent changes to mortgage rules.

In contrast, the Halifax office market is looking comparatively bright, buoyed by the fact that Nova Scotia is home to 78 head offices and a substantial number of regional offices—most of which call Halifax home.

All of Canada's major banks and several Fortune 500 companies have offices in the city. The Canada Revenue Agency has signed on to move into a new suburban office development, while financial services giant RBC has opened a new regional head office. Canadian Forces Base Halifax, Canada's largest military base, is attracting numerous defense companies to the area. And an offshore technology supply chain is arising around the Canadian Coast Guard regional headquarters, the Marine Security Operations Centre, and the Joint Rescue Coordination Centre.

Developers have responded to this concentration of head and regional offices and the influx of new industry clusters. New office buildings are coming on the market—along with a major new convention center/hotel/office complex slated for completion in 2016–2017. While the new buildings are expected to readily lure tenants, concerns exist that the older offices left behind will be rendered functionally obsolete.

Industrial development in and around Halifax has been relatively quiet, with some small developments underway but little more. Part of the reason is that newly announced shipbuilding contracts have thus far failed to deliver the anticipated boost to local job growth.

Local Market Opinion

In this year's survey, we asked participants to rank their local market on a number of variables associated with real estate performance. These results are important, given the desire of investors to look beyond more macro variables in search of opportunities in a wider set of markets.

A strong economy appears to bolster confidence in all sectors. Calgary and Edmonton respondents report feeling very good about the strength of the local economy, and this is translating into strong investor demand and capital availability. The majority of markets feel that capital is available and that development and redevelopment opportunities do exist in their market.

The widest divergence in responses is in the public/private investment category. Once again, the faster-growing economies have a more positive view on how the public and private sectors are working together.

Expected Best Bets in 2015

- Western Canada—especially Calgary, Edmonton, and Vancouver—will likely be the place to be in 2015.

- Retail in Greater Toronto and the Calgary urban core—especially where potential exists for income growth and redevelopment.

- Industrial in Calgary, Edmonton, and the western edge of Greater Toronto—in particular, properties designed to support distribution.

Exhibit 5-19 **Survey Respondents' View of Their Local Market**

	Average	Strength of local economy	Investor demand	Capital availability	Development/ redevelopment opportunities	Public/private investment	Local development community
			Fair	Good	Excellent		
Calgary	4.57	4.87	4.93	4.71	4.46	4.33	4.08
Edmonton	4.45	4.64	4.62	4.54	4.25	4.58	4.08
Toronto	3.94	3.61	4.17	4.18	3.64	3.82	4.23
Vancouver	3.94	3.77	4.50	4.43	3.69	3.38	3.85
Saskatoon	3.78	3.67	3.67	3.67	4.00	4.00	3.67
Ottawa	3.37	3.17	3.00	3.83	3.40	3.20	3.60
Montreal	3.28	3.00	3.50	3.50	3.33	2.89	3.44
Halifax	3.24	3.50	3.00	3.25	3.00	3.00	3.67
Winnipeg	3.14	3.17	3.33	3.17	3.00	3.17	3.00

Source: *Emerging Trends in Real Estate 2015* survey.

Note: Based on Canadian investors only.

- Land for both single-family home development and speculative industrial.

- Commercial and office space on the fringe of the current urban core—as long as it's at the right price.

- Purpose-built multiresidential in Greater Toronto, especially in core and transit corridors.

- Seniors' housing in good locations and managed by solid, trustworthy firms.

A Summary of Canadian Real Estate Trends

Canada's real estate market remains steady as the industry looks ahead to 2015. Economic growth in western Canada will continue to drive significant opportunity in Vancouver, Calgary, Edmonton, and Saskatoon in the residential, commercial, and office sectors. Toronto's housing market continues as a solid performer, while office and industrial sectors remain strong. Montreal looks to revitalize its treasured retail district to boost an increasingly condo-driven core. In Atlantic Canada, Halifax will build up commercial and office space while hoping for the residential market's sluggishness to end. And everywhere, industry players will search for opportunities in and around the city cores—capitalizing on the trend of urban migration that shows little sign of abating.

Interviewees

Ackman-Ziff Real Estate Group LLC
Gerald S. Cohen
Jason Kane
Russell Schildkraut
Simon Ziff

Aegis Property Group
Jim Kinzig

AEGON USA Realty Advisors Inc.
Donald P. Guarino Jr.

AEW Capital Management
Michael Acton
Dan Bradley
Marc Davidson
Pam Herbst
Robert Plumb

Agellan Commercial Real Estate Investment Trust
Frank Camenzuli

Allied Properties Real Estate Investment Trust
Michael Emory

Allstate Investments LLC
Edgar Alvarado

Alston & Bird LLP
Rosmarie Thurston

The Alterra Group of Companies
Robert Cooper

Altus Group Income Fund
Lou Iafrate

American Realty Advisors
Stanely Izeman

American Service and Recovery Group LLC
William Buchanan

Angelo Gordon
Reid Liffmann
Marc Maduras
Adam Schwartz
Gordon Whiting

APG Asset Management US Inc.
Steven Hason

Apollo Global Management LLC
Colburn J. Packard

ARA Finance
Tom MacManus

Arel Capital
Gabriel Bousbib
Teddy Schiff

Artemis Advisors LLC
Dale Anne Reiss

ASB Real Estate Investments
Larry Braithwaite

Aspac Developments Ltd.
Gary Wong

Avalon Bay
Kevin O'Shea

AXA Real Estate
Olivier Thoral

Axiometrics
Ronald Johnsey

Azrack & Co.
Joseph Azrack

Bank of America Merrill Lynch
Jeffrey D. Horowitz

Barclays Capital
P. Sheridan Schechner
Ross Smotrich

Basis Investment Group LLC
Mark K. Bhasin

Bay Hollow Associates
Alice Connell

Bentall Kennedy (Canada) LP
Remco Daal
Gary Whitelaw
Paul Zemla

Bentall Kennedy (US) LLP
Douglas Poutasse

BlackRock
Jack R. Chandler
Steve Cornet
Simon Treacy

The Blackstone Group
A.J. Agarwal

Blackstone Real Estate Advisors US
Frank Cohen

BMO Harris Bank
Hans C. Geyer
John Petrovski
John C. Wise

Board Member, Various Companies
Connie Moore

Boston Properties
Michael LaBelle
Owen D. Thomas

The Boulder Group
John Feeney

Brandywine Realty Trust
Jerry Sweeney

The Bristol Group Inc.
James Curtis

Brixmor Property Group
Michael V. Pappagallo

Brookdale Group
Dan Etheridge
David Hendrickson
Fred H. Henritze
Robert Turner

Brookfield Property Partners
Ric Clarke
Paul Schulman

Bucksbaum Retail Properties
John Bucksbaum

Build Toronto Inc.
Bill Bryck

Buzz McCoy Associates Inc.
Bowen H. "Buzz" McCoy

Cadillac Fairview Corp.
Cathal O'Connor

Canada Pension Plan Investment Board
Graeme Eadie

Canadian Apartment Properties Real Estate Investment Trust
Tom Schwartz

Canderel Management Inc.
Daniel Peritz

Canyon Capital Realty Advisors
Maria L. Stamolis

CapRidge Partners LLC
Steve LeBlanc

Capright
Jules "Jay" H. Marling

Carey Watermark Investors Inc.
Michael Medzigian

The Carlyle Group
Robert G. Stuckey

Carmel Partners
Dennis Markus
Ron Zeff

Cassidy Turley
Garrick Brown

CBRE
William C. Yowell

CBRE Commercial Tri-State Region
Mary Ann Tighe

CBRE Econometric Advisors
Jon Southard

CBRE Group Inc.
Tom Frye
Raymond Wong

CB Richard Ellis Ltd.
Ross Moore
John O'Bryan
Roelof van Dijk

Centerpoint Properties
James Clewlow

Charles River Realty Investors
Brian H. Kavoogian

China Healthcare Corp.
Charles A. "Chuck" Elcan

Christenson Advisors LLC
Kevin Christenson

Cigna Realty Advisors
Bill Carlson
John Clark
Nando Parete

Citi Private Equity Services
Michael Dwyer
Mark Suter

Cityscape Residential
Brian Cranor

Clapham Capital
Baxter Underwood

Clarett Group
Veronica Hackett

Clarion Partners
Hugh MacDonnell

Clark Street Development
Fritz L. Duda Jr.
Peter S. Eisenberg

CNL Commercial Real Estate
Paul Ellis

Colliers International
Craig Robinson

Colony Capital LLC
Richard B. Saltzman

Columbia Property Trust
James Fleming
Kevin Hoover
Neslon Mills

Compatriot Capital
Paul E. Rowsey III

Concert Properties Ltd.
David Podmore

The Concord Group
Richard M. Gollis

Connecticut Retirement Plants and Trust Funds (CRPTF)
Cherie Santos-Wuest

Cornerstone Real Estate Advisers
Scot Brown
Jim Clayton
Michael Gatley
David J. Reilly

CoStar Strategy
Hans Nordby

CRE Finance Council
Stephen M. Renna

CRL Senior Living
Douglas Cameron

Crow Holdings International
Harlan Crow
Anne Raymond

Crown Realty Partners
Michael Pittana

Cushman & Wakefield
James Carpenter
Steven A. Kohn

DDR Corp.
Dan Hurwitz

Desjardins Global Asset Management
Michel Bédard

Deutsche Asset & Wealth Management
Marc Feliciano
Todd Henderson
Mark Roberts

Distinguished Visiting Professor
David Shulman

Dividend Capital Group, University of Denver
Glenn Mueller

Donahue Schriber
Lawrence P. Casey

Dorsay Development Corp.
Geoffrey Grayhurst

Douglas Elliman
Faith Hope Consolo

DRA Advisors
Paul McEvoy Jr.

Dream Global REIT
Jane Gavan

Dream Office REIT
Michael Cooper

DREAM Unlimited Corp.
Jason Lester

DTH Capital
Steve Galiotos

Durum Properties Inc.
Jay Simmons

Eagle Realty Group
Mario San Marco
Tom Stapleton

Eastern Bank
David B. MacManus

Eastport Consulting
Susan Swindell Carter

Emigrant Bank
Pat Goldstein

Empire Communities Group
Paul Golini Jr.
Andrew Guizzetti
Daniel Guizzetti

Empire State Realty Trust
David Karp

Employee Retirement System of Texas
Robert Sessa

Epic Realty Partners Inc.
Gordon Thompson

Equity Residential
David Neithercut

Equus Capital Partners
Daniel M. DiLella Sr.

Essex Property Trust Inc.
Mike Schall

Fairview Investments
Barry Clarke

FG Asset Management
Edward A. Glickman

First American Title Insurance Co.
David J. Feldman

First Industrial Realty Trust Inc.
Jojo Yap

First Niagara Bank
Christophe P. Terlizzi

FirstKey Lending LLC
Simon Breedon

Fonds de Placement Immobilier Cominar
Todd Bechard
Sylvain Cossette

Fonds immobilier de solidarité FTQ
René Lamarche

Forest City Commercial Group
James Ratner

Fortis Properties Corp.
Terry K. Chaffey
Nora Duke
Stephen Hefferton

FPL Advisory
William Ferguson

The Furman Co.
Stephen P. Navarro

Geolo Capital
Anne Raymond

Gerding Edlen
Molly Bodonaro
Kelly Saito

Ginkgo Residential
Philip Payne

Glenborough LLC
Alan Shapiro

Goff Capital
John Goff

Goldman Sachs & Co.
Jeffrey A. Barclay

Grand Central Partnership
Fred Cerullo II
Duane Roggendorff
Marc Wurzel

Great Point Investors
Joseph Versaggi

GreenOak Real Estate
Sonny Kalsi

Greenpark Group of Companies
Carlo Baldassarra

Groupe Dallaire Inc.
Michel Berthelot

Grovesnor
Robert Hess

Grovesnor Americas
Eileen E. Marrinan

GTIS Partners
Steven Gorey

Guggenheim Partners
Kieran P. Quinn

GWL Realty Advisors Inc.
Paul Finkbeiner

Harrison Street Real Estate Capital
Thomas R. Errath

Hawkeye Partners LP
Bret Wilkerson

Heitman
Mary Ludgin

Helaba
Robert Becker
Aaron Jaffe
Mathias Wohlfahrt

Heron Group of Companies
Brad Foster
Hugh Heron

Hersha Hospitality Trust
Ashish Parikh
Jay Shah

Highwoods Properties
Edward J. Fritsch

Hilton Worldwide
Kevin Jacobs
Chris Nassetta

Hines
Kurt Hartman
Ken Hubbard

Hopewell Development Corp.
Don Larke

Hopewell Residential Communities Inc.
Lesley Conway

Hyde Street Holdings LLC
Patricia R. Healy

ICSC
Michael P. Kercheval

IDI Gazeley
Linda Booker

IDR Index Management LP
Charles R. Purse
Gary Zdolshek

Inland Private Capital Corp.
Rahul Sehgal

Institutional Real Estate Inc.
Geoffrey Dohrmann

Intracorp Group
Don Forsgren

Invesco Real Estate
Tim Bellman
Scott Dennis

Island Capital Group
Robert Lieber

iStar Financial
Nina Matis

ITC Group of Companies
Doug MacFarlane

Ivanhoe Cambridge Inc.
Sylvain Fortier
William R.C. Tresham

JLA LLC
Steve Utley

J.P. Morgan Asset Management
Nancy Brown
Anne Cole
Wayne Comer
Michael Hudgins
Mike Kelly
Brian Nottage
Hilary Spann

John Hancock
Joseph Shaw

KeyBanc Real Estate Capital
Angela Mago

Kimco Realty Corp.
Conor Flynn
David Henry

Kimpton Hotels & Restaurants
Joe Long

KingSett Capital Inc.
Jon Love

KKR
Ralph Rosenberg

Klingbeil Capital Management
Kevin Kaz

KMK Capital Inc.
Kevin King

Korpacz Realty Advisors Inc.
Peter Korpacz

Lachman Associates
Leanne Lachman

Ladder Capital Finance LLC
Greta Guggenheim
Michael Mazzei

LaSalle Hotel Properties
Michael D. Barnello

LaSalle Investment Management
Zelick Altman
Jacques Gordon
Jason Kern

Liberty Property Trust
Michael T. Hagan
William Hankowsky

Linneman Associates and American Land Fund
Peter Linneman

Lubert-Adler
Dean S. Adler

Madison Homes
Miguel Singer

M.A.M. Group Inc.
Mauro Baldassarra

Manulife Financial
Joseph Shaw

Manulife Real Estate Funds
Catherine Barbaro
Tim Blair
David Shaw
Ted Willcocks

Martek
Charlie Oliver

The Mathews Co.
Bert Mathews

Mattamy Homes Ltd.
Brian Johnston

MDF Capital
Michael D. Fascitelli

Melcor REIT
Darin Rayburn

Menkes Development Group
Peter Menkes

Mesa Development
Richard A. Hanson

MetLife Real Estate Investors
Chuck Davis
Mark H. Wilsmann

Metrolinx
Michael Sutherland

The Metrontario Group
Lawrie Lubin

Metrus Properties
Robert De Gasperis

Metzler North America
Donald Wise

Moody's Investors Service
Merrie S. Frankel

Morgan Stanley & Co.
Jim Collins
John Klopp
Grant Murray
Candice Todd

Murray Hill Properties
Norman Sturner

National Association of Real Estate Investment Trusts
Steven Wechsler

New Tower Trust Co.
Brent A. Palmer

Newcastle Ltd.
Kent Swanson

Newport Capital Partners
Derrick McGavic

Next Realty LLC
Andy Hochberg
Alex Katz

Ninety Degree Enterprises
Guy F. Jaquier

Noble Investment Group
Jim Conley

NorthWest Healthcare Properties REIT
Peter Riggin

NorthWest International Healthcare Properties REIT
Paul Dalla Lana

Northwestern Mutual
David Clark

Northwood Investors
John Kukral

NPV Advisors
David Walden
John Wrzensinksi

Ohana Real Estate Investors
Sarah Mancuso

ONNI Group of Companies

Orlando Corp.
Nick Fuda
Bill O'Rourke

Otéra Capital
Alfonso Graceffa
Edmondo Marandola

Oxford Properties Group Inc.
Blake Hutcheson

Pan-Canadian Mortgage Group Inc.
Joel McLean

Paramount Group Inc.
Albert Behler

Park Hill Real Estate Group
Michael Stark

Parkway
Jason Bates

Partners Group (USA) Inc.
Mark Degner
Marc Weiss

Pearlmark Real Estate Partners
Stephen R. Quazzo

Penney Group Inc.
Gail Penney

Pension Real Estate Association (PREA)
Greg MacKinnon

Penwood Real Estate Investment Management LLC
Richard H. Chase
John M. Hurley
Karen A. Nista

Piedmont Office Realty Trust
Donald A. Miller

Plazacorp Retail REIT
Kevin Salsberg

PM Realty Group
John S. Dailey

PNC Real Estate Finance
William G. Lashbrook

Polygon Homes Ltd.
Robert Bruno
Neil Chrystal

Post Properties Inc.
David P. Stockert

PREA
Greg MacKinnon

Preferred Apartment Communities Inc.
Leonard A. Silverstein
John A. Williams

Preferred Capital Advisors
Daniel Corfee
Benjamin Faubion

Pretium Partners LLC
Curt Schade

Principal Enterprise Capital
Dan Schulte
Emily Slovitt

Principal Real Estate Investors
Russ Beecher
John Frandson
Michael J. Lara

Prologis
Chris Caton
Hamid Moghadam

Prudential Global Real Estate Securities Fund
Marc Halle

Prudential Real Estate Investors
Kevin R. Smith

Public Sector Pension Investment Board
Neil Cunningham

Pure Industrial Real Estate Trust
Francis Tam

QIC
Matthew Strotton

Quadrant
Thomas Mattinson

RBC Capital Markets
Carolyn Blair
Dan Giaquinto
David Tweedie

Real Estate Capital Partners
Paul Doocy
Sylvia Gross
Jeremy Katz
Karen Shewer

The Real Estate Roundtable
Jeffrey DeBoer

Real Property Association of Canada
Michael Brooks

RealNet Canada Inc.
George Carras

Redbourne Group
Michel Bouchard

REIS Inc.
Ryan Severino

RioCan Real Estate Investment Trust
Rags Davloor
Ed Sonshine
Fred Waks

RLJ Lodging Trust
Ross H. Bierken

Rohit Group of Companies
Russell Dauk

Rosen Consulting Group
Kenneth Rosen

Sabra Healthcare REIT Inc.
Talya Nevo-Hacohen

Schribner Realty Group
Patrick S. Donahue

Scotia Capital Inc.
Stephen Sender

Seavest Healthcare Properties
Shak Chowdhury
Douglas Ray
John Winter

Seven Hills Properties
Luis A. Belmonte

Shelter Rock Capital Advisors
Walter Stackler

Shorenstein Properties LLC
Glenn A. Shannon

Siegel-Gallagher Inc.
Patrick Gallagher

Silverpeak Real Estate Partners
Rodolpho Amboss

Silverstein WEC Development
Larry Silverstein

Skanska USA Commercial Development Inc.
Catherine Pfeiffenberger

The Sorbara Group
Edward Sorbara

Starwood Capital Group
Carl B. Tash

Starwood Property Group
Marcos Alvarado
Jerry C. Silvey

State Teachers Retirement System of Ohio
Stanton West

Sunstone Hotel Investors Inc.
John Arabia

SVP Investments Glenborough LLC
Alan Shapiro

T.A. Associates Realty
Nilesh Bubna

Taubman Centers
Robert Taubman

TCR
Ken Valach

Thibault, Messier, Savard, and Associates Inc.
Martin Galarneau

TIAA-CREF
Robert Villamanga

TIAA-CREF Asset Management
Richard Coppola

TIAA Henderson Real Estate
James Martha

Tideline Partners
Lev Gershahn

Toronto Port Lands Co.
Michael Kraljevic

The Townsend Group
Jennifer Young

Trepp LLC
Matt Anderson

True North Apartment REIT
Leslie Veiner

Turner Construction Co.
Darin Postma

Unaffiliated
Jeff Blackman
Jeff Browning

UBS Global Asset Management (Americas) Inc.
Lee S. Saltzman

UBS Realty Investors LLC
Gary Gowdy
Matthew Lynch

United States Steel and Carnegie Pension Fund
Ione S.V. Wilsmann

University of California
Gloria Gil

Urban America
Thomas Kennedy

Urban Properties
John Breitinger

USAA Real Estate Company
Len O'Donnell

Valenica Group
John Keeling

Vermilion Development
Dave Cocagne

Voyager Capital
Curtis Feeny

Vulcan Real Estate
Lori Mason Curran
Ada Healey

W.P. Carey Inc.
Trevor P. Bond
Tom Zacharias

Walton Street Capital LLC
Jeffrey Quicksilver

Wangard
Stewart Wangard

Wells Fargo Real Estate Banking Group
Wayne Brandt

Westbank Projects Corp.
Judy Leung

Westfield Group
Peter Lowy
Mark Stefanek

Westport Capital Partners
Russ Bernard

Sponsoring Organizations

PwC real estate practice assists real estate investment advisers, real estate investment trusts, public and private real estate investors, corporations, and real estate management funds in developing real estate strategies; evaluating acquisitions and dispositions; and appraising and valuing real estate. Its global network of dedicated real estate professionals enables it to assemble for its clients the most qualified and appropriate team of specialists in the areas of capital markets, systems analysis and implementation, research, accounting, and tax.

Global Real Estate Leadership Team

R. Byron Carlock Jr.
National Real Estate Practice Leader
Dallas, Texas, U.S.A.

Mitchell M. Roschelle
National Real Estate Advisory Practice Leader
New York, New York, U.S.A.

Richard Fournier
National Real Estate Assurance Leader
New York, New York, U.S.A.

Christine Lattanzio
Real Estate Tax Leader
New York, New York, U.S.A.

Kees Hage
Global Real Estate Leader
Luxembourg, Luxembourg

Uwe Stoschek
Global Real Estate Tax Leader
European, Middle East & Africa Real Estate Leader
Berlin, Germany

K.K. So
Asia Pacific Real Estate Tax Leader
Hong Kong, China

Craig Hughes
U.K. and Global SWF Real Estate Leader
London, U.K.

Frank Magliocco
National Real Estate Leader
Toronto, Ontario, Canada

www.pwc.com

The mission of the Urban Land Institute is to provide leadership in the responsible use of land and in creating and sustaining thriving communities worldwide. ULI is committed to

■ Bringing together leaders from across the fields of real estate and land use policy to exchange best practices and serve community needs;

■ Fostering collaboration within and beyond ULI's membership through mentoring, dialogue, and problem solving;

■ Exploring issues of urbanization, conservation, regeneration, land use, capital formation, and sustainable development;

■ Advancing land use policies and design practices that respect the uniqueness of both built and natural environments;

■ Sharing knowledge through education, applied research, publishing, and electronic media; and

■ Sustaining a diverse global network of local practice and advisory efforts that address current and future challenges.

Established in 1936, the Institute today has more than 32,000 members worldwide, representing the entire spectrum of the land use and development disciplines. Professionals represented include developers, builders, property owners, investors, architects, public officials, planners, real estate brokers, appraisers, attorneys, engineers, financiers, academics, students, and librarians.

ULI relies heavily on the experience of its members. It is through member involvement and information resources that ULI has been able to set standards of excellence in development practice. The Institute has long been recognized as one of the world's most respected and widely quoted sources of objective information on urban planning, growth, and development.

Patrick L. Phillips
Global Chief Executive Officer, Urban Land Institute

Kathleen B. Carey
Chief Content Officer

ULI Center for Capital Markets and Real Estate
Anita Kramer
Senior Vice President
www.uli.org/capitalmarketscenter

Urban Land Institute
1025 Thomas Jefferson Street, NW
Suite 500 West
Washington, DC 20007
202-624-7000
www.uli.org